WHO
DONE IT?

Publications International, Ltd.

Cover art: Shutterstock.com

Puzzle constructors: Cihan Altay, Myles Callum, Philip Carter, Andrew Clarke, Barry Clarke, Adrian Fisher, Luke Haward, Shelly Hazard, Dick Hess, Marilynn Huret, Stephen Ryder, Paul Seaburn, Terry Stickels, Nicole Sulgit, Wayne Robert Williams, Alex Willmore

Puzzle illustrators: Helem An, Chris Gattorna, Robin Humer, Nicole H. Lee, Jay Sato, Shavan Spears, Jen Torche

Louis Weber, CEO
Publications International, Ltd.
8140 Lehigh Avenue
Morton Grove, Illinois 60053

Permission is never granted for commercial purposes.

ISBN: 978-1-68022-313-2

Manufactured in China.

Investigate, Deduce, Solve!

Did you want to be a detective when you were a kid? Were you the person who solved "everyday" mysteries when others were stumped? Now you have a chance to relive those days! The mind stretchers in this book will let you put on your thinking cap, make deductions, and use all your logic skills to solve close to 200 puzzles.

We've assembled a variety of mind stretchers here. There are word puzzles, number puzzles, memory puzzles, and reading comprehension puzzles. You'll need verbal, numerical, and visual acuity. You'll solve some with bursts of inspiration while others will require hard work as you track down a chain of logic. All of them will stretch your brain and help you challenge yourself!

Don't worry if you find yourself getting stuck from time to time. Answers are located at the back of the book when you need a helpful boost.

So when you're ready to go on a Treasure Hunt, decipher a cryptogram, untangle a logic puzzle, unscramble an anagram, or figure out a Spy Fly puzzle, just open the book. You'll find a puzzle to challenge yourself on each page. They'll keep your brain sharp even as you enjoy yourself.

These mind stretchers can be done anytime, anywhere. So if you have time for a quick puzzle challenge while you're having coffee, riding the train to work, or waiting in line, pull out *Brain Games®: Who Done It?* and start solving!

MOTEL HIDEOUT

A thief hides out in one of the 45 motel rooms listed in the chart below. The motel's in-house detective received a sheet of four clues, signed "The Holiday Thief." Using these clues, the detective found the room number within 15 minutes—but by that time, the thief had fled. Can you find the thief's motel room quicker?

1. Of the 2 digits in the room number, one of them is an odd number and the other is even. *odd/even*

2. The second digit in the room number is more than twice as large as the first digit. *1x/2x*

3. The room number cannot be evenly divided by 7.

4. If the 2 digits in the room number changed positions, it would still be a room number in the motel as listed in the chart.

51	52	53	54	55	56	57	58	59
41	42	43	44	45	46	47	48	49
31	32	33	34	35	36	37	38	39
21	22	23	24	25	26	27	28	29
11	12	13	14	15	16	17	18	19

Answers on page 169.

PRIME SUSPECT

The police have drawn up a list of prime suspect descriptions for a recent bank robbery. However, due to a clerical error, although each item is in the correct column, only one entry in each column is correctly positioned. The following facts are true about the correct order.

1. Yellow is one row below medium and somewhere above mauve.

2. Thin is 2 rows above Spanish.

3. Hunched is 3 places below English.

4. White is somewhere above dark and 2 places above fat.

5. Italian is 2 places above purple.

6. Brown is one row below both yellow and African.

7. Cream is immediately below purple but 3 places below none.

Can you find the correct nationality, hair color, coat color, and build for each suspect?

	Nationality	Hair	Coat	Build
1	English	none	green	slim
2	Italian	white	yellow	thin
3	Spanish	red	mauve	fat
4	Mexican	gray	blue	round
5	African	brown	purple	medium
6	Chinese	dark	cream	hunched

Answers on page 169.

LIAR'S LOGIC!

Decipher the statements below using the following information to figure out who is lying and who is telling the truth. There are 2 truth tellers, and 3 liars.

Person A says person E is lying.

Person B says person C is lying.

Person C says person B is lying.

Person D says person B is telling the truth.

Person E says person C is telling the truth.

MYSTERY IN ENGLAND

Read the mystery below, and see how good a detective you are!

While visiting Lord Wisenberry of Eaglethorpe, in his English mansion, you decide to go exploring. In the basement, you accidentally lock yourself in a dusty storage room. There's only one door and no windows. The door key is hanging on a hook high on the wall, but no matter how much you jump, you can't reach it. You try calling for help, but everyone is at the other end of the mansion.

The only items in the room are a deck of playing cards with the king of spades missing, a broken cardboard box holding a set of 24 encyclopedias from 1934, and a dirty blue rug. How will you get out of the room?

Answers on page 169.

PASSWORD MAKER
(PART I)

Most of us have a computer these days, and most programs require a password. What's your method of coming up with one? To make the password easy to remember, most people use some combination of their initials and birthday. But that also makes it easier for someone else to guess. One good method is to put together two unrelated words, like JOKER CAMEL or TRUMPET ANKLE. No need to work hard at that, though, because we're going to give you 10 good passwords at no charge! Read this list over a few times, then turn the page.

ADVICE KETTLE

PIANO LOBSTER

BELIEF HAMMER

FREEDOM ELEPHANT

CONCEPT SALAMANDER

PRESTIGE NINETEEN

FLUTTER CAMPUS

QUOTATION ORANGE

COWBOY GOLDEN

MOUNTAIN CYMBAL

PASSWORD MAKER (PART II)

(Don't look at this until you've looked at the words on page 7!)

Now that you've looked at the list for a few minutes, here are the passwords again, in random order. Can you remember at least 8 word pairs?

_____ GOLDEN

FREEDOM _____

_____ ORANGE

FLUTTER _____

_____ CYMBAL

ADVICE _____

_____ LOBSTER

PRESTIGE _____

_____ HAMMER

CONCEPT _____

Answers on page 169.

NAUGHTY STUDENTS

Four students are in front of the principal for breaking rules. The principal's secretary has made a list of the crime and designated punishment for each student but has mixed up the details. Although each item is in the correct column, only one item in each column correctly is positioned. The following facts are true about the correct order:

1. Goof is one place below Colin and two places below stealing books.

2. Forfeiting sport is two places above talking back.

3. Cleaning windows is one place below Finkel but one place above Denzil.

Can you give the correct name, surname, crime, and punishment for each position?

	Name	Surname	Crime	Punishment
1	Andy	Everong	eating in class	cleaning windows
2	Bernard	Finkel	breaking chairs	mopping floors
3	Colin	Goof	talking back	forfeiting sport
4	Denzil	Harrow	stealing books	extra assignments

Answers on page 169.

THE SCRAMBLED DETECTIVE

Sometimes the scrambled detective gets so excited when he's on the case that his words get scrambled. Help his assistant figure out what to do next. Fill in the blanks in the detective's instructions with words that are anagrams (rearrangements) of the capitalized words.

"To VOLES _____ this dastardly crime, we need to look for EVEN DICE _____. Let's start by looking for FERN STRIPING _____, PROTON FITS _____, and BRIEFS_____."

ADDAGRAM

This puzzle functions exactly like an anagram with an added step: In addition to being scrambled, each word below is missing the same letter. Discover the missing letter, then unscramble the words. When you do, you'll reveal four words related to detection.

CONFERS

HEFT

AXE MEN

STATE GIVEN

Answers on page 169.

GEMSTONE MATH

There are 5 types of gems. There is 1 gem of the first type, 2 of the second type, 3 of the third type, 4 of the fourth type, and 5 of the fifth type. From the information given below, can you tell how many gemstones there are of each kind?

There are 3 more emeralds than there are aquamarines. There is an even number of opals and an odd number of peridots. There are fewer agates than aquamarines.

DETECTIVE'S TOOLKIT

The detective was putting together the tools she needed. Can you determine the order of the 6 tools gathered from the information below?

The magnifying glass was one of the first three things gathered.

The notepad was not gathered immediately before or after the pencil, nor was it found last.

The fingerprint kit was found right before the flashlight.

The pencil was found third or fourth.

The magnifying glass was put in the kit, then three other items, and then the measuring tape.

The flashlight was found right before the measuring tape.

Answers on page 169.

DELIVERY DILEMMA

The newspaper delivery boy has mixed up his list of newspaper names and their intended recipients. Although each item is in the correct column, only one item in each column is correctly positioned. The following facts are certain about the correct order:

1. Daily is somewhere above Illingworth, which is not above Early.

2. Mail is one place below Horsefield and one place above Morning.

3. Clarion is not at 4.

4. Fallon is two places above Express and one above Weekly.

Can you determine the correct recipient and two-word newspaper title for each position?

	Recipient	Title 1	Title 2
1	Fallon	*Morning*	*Mail*
2	Graham	*Daily*	*Platform*
3	Horsefield	*Early*	*Clarion*
4	Illingworth	*Weekly*	*Tablet*
5	Jameson	*New*	*Express*

Answers on page 170.

RELATIONS PROBLEM

A man points to a woman and says, "That woman's mother-in-law and my mother-in-law are mother and daughter—in some order." What ways can the woman be related to the man?

VISUAL SEQUENCE

Which of the lettered figures below continues this sequence?

A.   B.   C.   D.   E.   F.

Answers on page 170.

SPY FLY

As an international spy, your mission is to travel from your headquarters at Seth Castle to your safe house at Faro. To disguise your trail, you must stop once—and only once—at each airport. See if you can find the cheapest route for your trip. Less than $260 would make you a Steady Sleuth; less than $240, a Cool Operator; less than $220, a Crafty Agent. If you can make it on $200, then you're a Super Spy!

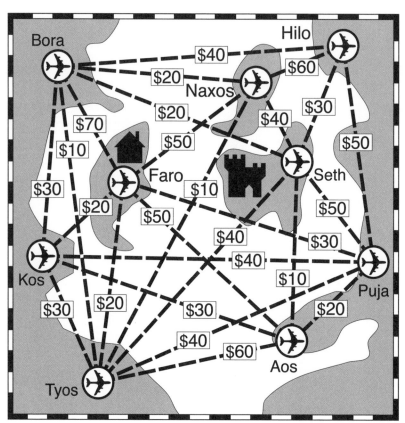

Answers on page 170.

RIDDLE

A man drives into a parking lot in Lincolnwood, Illinois, gets out, securely locks and tests all the car doors and windows, and goes into the local bank. When he returns 20 minutes later he finds that a cat, which he has never seen before, is curled up asleep and contented on the back seat. All the doors and windows are still securely locked and the car is exactly how he had left it prior to entering to the bank, apart from the cat.

How did the cat get into the car?

FAMOUS DETECTIVE SCRAMBLE

The left column contains the scrambled names of five famous fictional detectives. The right column contains the authors who created them. Unscramble the names and then match each detective to its creator!

Detectives:

1. HEMLOCKS RESLOSH

2. SLAM SIMPER

3. D. AUSPICE UNTUG

4. FOOL NEWER

5. MONKEY ILLSHINE

Authors:

A. TEX TOURS

B. FORAGES NUT

C. AGHAST CHAIRTIE

D. ADAGE LONER LAP

E. ATRULY HONOR DANCE

Answers on page 170.

MEND THE BRIDGES

Rain has swept through the entire county, flooding all the bridges indicated by circles. Your job is to travel to each location—A through I, in any order—by restoring only 2 of the bridges.

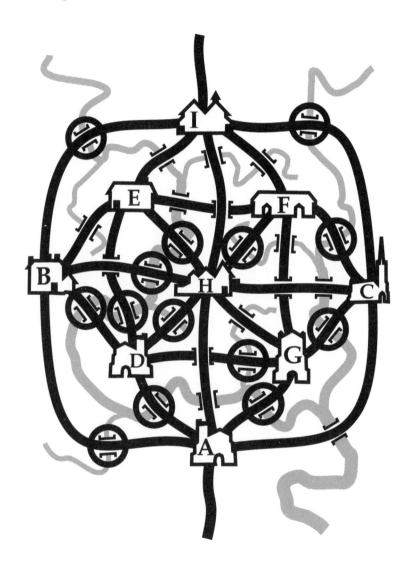

Answers on page 170.

HOW'S YOUR RECALL?
(PART I)

Study these items for a minute, then turn the page for a memory challenge.

Opera Glasses

Basketball Hoop

Toy Car

Taj Mahal

Camp Tent

Gumball Machine

Treasure Chest

Key Chain

Picture Frame

HOW'S YOUR RECALL?
(PART II)

Do not look at this until you have read the previous page! Check off the 2-word captions you saw on the previous page:

___ MOUNT FUJI

___ LOTTERY MACHINE

✓ KEY CHAIN

___ VERDI'S AIDA

✓ CAMP TENT

✓ BASKETBALL COURT

___ HORSE OPERA

✓ PICTURE FRAME

✓ CAMP TENT

___ TAPE MEASURE

___ PINKING SHEARS

___ HULA HOOP

✓ OPERA GLASSES

___ FISHING ROD

✓ TREASURE CHEST

___ EIFFEL TOWER

Answers on page 170.

ROBBER RIDDLE

Cryptograms are messages in substitution code. Break the code to read the riddle and its answer. For example, THE SMART CAT might become FVO QWGDF JGF if F is substituted for T, V for H, O for E, and so on.

AKZ FMF UKG OIDDGO UBNG B DBUK

DGHIOG CIMSC UI UKG DBSN?

DGWBXVG KG ABSUGF UI QBNG VXOG KG

KBF B WPGBS CGUBABZ.

RACE TO THE TRUTH

Can you determine the order of the 7 runners in the race based on the information below?

Val came in directly ahead of Dayton, but not in the top 3. Sloane didn't place in the top 3 either, but was happy to be somewhere ahead of nemesis Blaise. Misha was either 2nd or 4th. Cassidy was directly behind Addison for most of the race, but another runner came between them in the final standings. Cassidy and Val were separated by 2 runners.

1 Addison   5 Blaise   Val, Dayton
2 Misha   6 Val   Sloane
3 Cassidy   7 Dayton   Blaise
4 Sloane

Answers on page 171.

MRS. SMITH'S DAUGHTERS

Jane, Anna, Kate, and Sarah are Mrs. Smith's 4 daughters. Each daughter has a different hair color (black, blond, brown, or red) and a different eye color (blue, brown, green, or hazel). Using the information given, try to determine not only each daughter's hair and eye color but also whether she is one, two, three, or four years old.

1. The girl with black hair is younger than Sarah.

2. Of Jane and Anna, one has brown hair and the other has brown eyes but neither is the oldest or youngest.

3. Kate does not have hazel eyes.

4. The blond is younger than the girl with green eyes but older than Anna.

		JANE	ANNA	KATE	SARAH	HAIR				EYES			
						BLACK	BLOND	BROWN	RED	BLUE	BROWN	GREEN	HAZEL
4 YEARS OLD		X	X	X	O	X	X	X	O	X	X	O	X
3 YEARS OLD		O	X	X	X	X	O	X	X	X	O	X	X
2 YEARS OLD		X	O	X	X	X	X	O	X	X	X	X	O
1 YEAR OLD		X	X	O	X	O	X	X	X	O	X	X	X
EYES	BLUE	X	X	O	X	O	X	X	X				
	BROWN	O	X	X	X	X	O	X	X				
	GREEN	X	X	X	O	X	X	X	O				
	HAZEL	X	O	X	X	X	X	O	X				
HAIR	BLACK	X	X	O	X								
	BLOND	O	X	X	X								
	BROWN	X	O	X	X								
	RED	X	X	X	O								

Answers on page 171.

21

OFF COLOR

A family has hired several friends to paint parts of their house. However, they have managed to write down their plans incorrectly. Although each item is in the correct column, only one item in each column is correctly positioned. The following facts are certain about the correct order:

1. Keith is not second.

2. The hall is one place above purple.

3. The stairway is one place below Keith.

4. The hall is not first.

5. Red is one place above Jenny.

Can you give the location, color, and painter's name for each position?

	Location	Color	Painter
1	kitchen	red	Sid
2	bathroom	yellow	Jenny
3	hall	black	Keith
4	stairway	purple	Lorna

Answers on page 171.

RESTAURANT RIDDLE

There are 8 restaurants, 4 on each side of the road. From the information given below, figure out which restaurant is which.

As you walk down the street, the Polish restaurant is the first one you pass on one side of the street. The Thai place, which is not on the same side of the street as the Polish restaurant, is directly across from the Irish pub. The Italian restaurant is on the same side of the street as the seafood restaurant, but there are two other restaurants between them. The Greek place and the Irish pub are adjacent to each other on the same side of the street. The deli is across from the Italian restaurant. The French bistro is on the opposite side of the street from the Polish restaurant, but not directly across from it.

LOGICAL HATS

Each of 3 logicians A, B, and C wears a hat with a positive whole number on it. The number on one hat is the sum of the numbers on the other two. Each logician can see the numbers on the other 2 hats but not on their own. They have this information and are asked in turn to identify their own number.

A: "I don't know my number."

B: "My number is 15."

What numbers are on A and C?

Answers on page 171.

TREASURE HUNT

The treasure hunter visited eight cities, finding a clue in each one that led her to the treasure in the final city. Can you put the list of the eight cities she visited in order, using the information below?

The three cities with names that began with the letter C were visited one after the other. *Copenhagen, Caracas, Canberra*

Dakar was one of the first four cities visited; the other African capital on the list was one of the final four cities.

Budapest was visited immediately before Vientiane, which was not where the treasure was found.

Copenhagen was one of the first three cities visited.

Neither Caracas nor Dakar was the first city visited.

Nairobi was visited immediately after Kingston.

One city separated the visit to Canberra and the later visit to Budapest.

Three cities separated the visit to the Jamaican capital from the earlier visit to the city in Australia.

1 Copenhagen
2 Caracas
3 Canberra
4 Dakar

5 Budapest
6 Vientiane
7 Kingston
8 Nairobi

Answers on page 171.

LOTTERY TICKETS

Lou Zer was in charge of the lottery pool at the office. He bought the same number of lottery tickets every week at a dollar apiece. Lou and 9 coworkers each put equal amounts into the pool. One week, 2 people felt unlucky and dropped out, so Lou convinced the rest to put in another dollar so he could still buy the same number of lottery tickets. How many lottery tickets did Lou buy every week?

10 participants

SEQUENCING

Study this sequence:

> Radiant, bravery, dioxide, obelisk, obscure, mandate

Of the options below, which should come next?

> Bonanza, inwards, winsome, surmise, routine

Answers on page 172.

LIAR'S LOGIC!

Decipher the statements below using the following information to figure out who is lying and who is telling the truth. There are 3 truth tellers and 2 liars.

Person A says person B is telling the truth.

Person B says person D is lying.

Person C says person A is lying.

Person D says person C is telling the truth.

Person E says person A is telling the truth.

CRYPTO-LOGIC

Each of the numbers in the sequence below represents a letter. Use the mathematical clues to determine which number stands for which letter and reveal the encrypted word.

Hint: Remember that a / indicates divided by, and that all sums in parentheses must be done first.

7 3 2 1 5

Clues:	D = R − 3	2D = P	½ G = H
	D + I = 7	10 − P = 2	
	2G = D	(R + I) / 2 = T	

Answers on page 172.

COOL CAFÉ

In the Cool Café, the waiter has written down his orders incorrectly. Each item in the chart is in the correct column, and all the numbers in the first column are correctly positioned, but only one item in each of the remaining columns is correctly positioned. Using the clues below, can you correctly identify the surname, drink, and number of sugars for each order?

1. The latte or the coffee gets either 0 or 1 sugar.

2. Second to receive their order is Aviary, who has neither 1 nor 3 sugars and did not order a latte.

3. Just after Aviary is neither Bloggs nor Dribble, but whoever it is receives 0 sugar in either tea or mocha.

	Surname	Drink	Sugars
1	Aviary	tea	0
2	Bloggs	coffee	1
3	Crumple	latte	2
4	Dribble	mocha	3

Answers on page 172.

SOCK DRAWER

Tiny Tom can barely reach into the top drawer of his highboy where he keeps his socks. He knows he has 11 pairs of black socks and 6 pairs of brown socks scattered in the drawer with no pairs knotted together.

How many socks would he have to pull out of the drawer in order to ensure that he gets a matching pair?

EQUALIZING HEADS

There are 23 ordinary coins lying flat on a table in a completely dark room. Besides the 15 that have heads up, 8 have tails up. You are in the room and must separate the coins into 2 groups, each of which has the same number of heads up. You may turn over coins but you cannot distinguish heads from tails in any way. No tricks are involved here.

Answers on page 172.

IT'S A SHORE THING (PART I)

This beach has an unusual entrance "fee": Before you can use the beach, you've got to take a memory test. Study this picture for 2 minutes, then turn the page and answer the 10 questions to earn your beach permit for the day!

IT'S A SHORE THING (PART II)

(Do not read this until you have read the previous page!)

The beach patrol asks you the following questions:

1. What toy were the kids in the water throwing? _Fresby_

2. What was the girl with the braids holding? _shell_

3. What was the name of the lotion the woman was putting on her arm?
goop

4. What was the design on the swimsuit that same woman was wearing?
stripes

5. What kind of animal was the float in the water shaped like? _alligator_

6. What was the name of the sailboat? _Breeze_

7. What had the angler caught? _Boton_

8. What 3 types of clothing were worn by the man holding hands with his wife?
hat, short, Tshi

9. What does the lifeguard have slung over his arm? _megaphone_

10. How many birds were in the picture? _3_

Answers on page 172.

MEND THE BRIDGES

...ain has swept through the entire county, flooding all the bridges indicated by
...rcles. Your job is to travel to each location—A through I, in any order—by restor-
...g only 2 of the bridges.

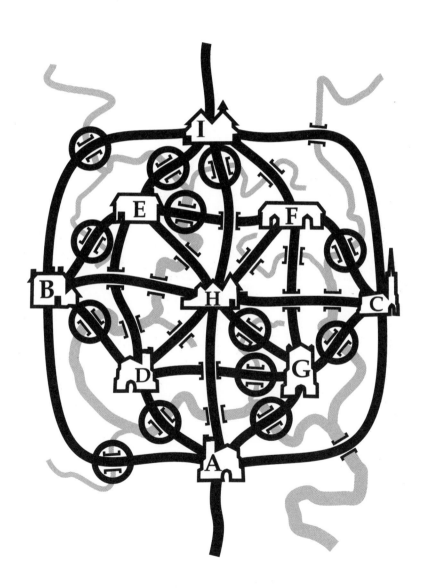

Answers on page 173.

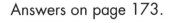

WILD WEST

The Western cattle trail was notorious for fights among the cowhands. The leader noted the names of the 6 hands who were shot on the journey, but on reaching his destination he found that he had mixed up the order and details. Although each detail is in the correct column, only 1 entry in each of the 4 columns is correctly positioned. Can you find the correct name, surname, location, and firearm involved in each duel and determine the correct order in which they took place?

1. San Antonio is 3 places above the Golden Boy.

2. Hitchcock is somewhere above Lightning and 2 places above the Derringer.

3. Earp is 2 places below Fort Griffin.

4. Kid is 1 row below both Butch and Colby.

5. Fingers is immediately below Earp but 3 places below Garrett.

6. Butch is 1 row below the Winchester and somewhere above Cat.

7. The Peacemaker is 2 rows above Dodge City.

	Name	Surname	Location	Firearm
1	Abel	Garrett	San Antonio	Schofield
2	Butch	Hitchcock	Fort Griffin	Peacemaker
3	Cat	Indiana	Dodge City	Derringer
4	Drew	James	Ogallala	Cavalry
5	Earp	Kid	Colby	Winchester
6	Fingers	Lightning	Red River	Golden Boy

Answers on page 173.

GEMSTONE MATH

There are 5 types of gems. There is 1 gem of the first type, 2 of the second type, 3 of the third type, 4 of the fourth type, and 5 of the fifth type. From the information given below, can you tell how many gemstones there are of each kind?

There are 2 more rubies than there are sapphires. There are fewer pearls than sapphires. There are 3 more garnets than there are emeralds. There are more rubies than garnets.

SEQUENCING

Can you complete the sequence below?

The detective is tracking down some stolen gems. She has found the pearls in the city of Edinburgh, the opals in the city of Oslo, and the garnets in the city of Athens. Where are the rubies most likely to be found?

A. Ulan Bator

B. Reykjavik

C. Yerevan

D. Bern

Answers on page 173.

SPY FLY

As an international spy, your mission is to travel from your headquarters at Seth Castle to your safe house at Faro. To disguise your trail, you must stop once—and only once—at each airport. See if you can find the cheapest route for your trip. Less than $280 would make you a Steady Sleuth; less than $260, a Cool Operator; less than $240, a Crafty Agent. If you can make it on $220, then you're a Super Spy!

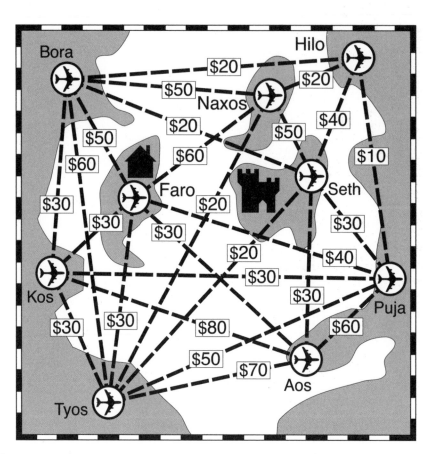

$\bigoplus$ = Airport

🏰 = Start

🏠 = Finish

Answers on page 173.

RACE TO THE TRUTH

Can you determine the order of the 7 runners in the race based on the information below?

Casey won one of the top three medals. Amisha was either 2nd or 6th. Alex was directly behind her. Leticia came up from behind to pass first Chris and then Tim, but she couldn't get ahead of Casey. Eric was somewhere ahead of Alex but somewhere behind Chris.

THE ANSWER'S ON THE MONEY

There is a sum of money that can be equally divided among 5, 17, or 23 people. What is the least amount of money in whole dollars this sum could be?

Answers on page 173.

TREASURE HUNT

The treasure hunter visited eight cities, finding a clue in each one that led her to the treasure in the final city. Can you put the list of the eight cities she visited in order, using the information below?

She went directly from the capital city of one of the smallest countries in Europe to the capital city of the largest country by area in the world.

She went from Tashkent directly to the capital of the United States.

Moscow's clue led her immediately to Oslo.

Montevideo was not one of the first four cities she visited, but she did not find the treasure there.

There were two cities between her visit to Washington, D.C., and her visit to Ankara.

There were exactly four cities between her visit to Luxembourg and her visit to New Delhi.

The capital of Norway was one of the first four cities she visited.

Answers on page 173.

A CAN-DO CANDLE ATTITUDE

It's birthday time at the Shady Rest Village for Feisty Grandmas and Grandpas. Mona is turning 100. The other residents gave Dan $100 to buy Mona a variety of cool candles for the cake that Kate is baking. At the store, Dan found cheap candles for 50 cents, nice candles for $5.50, and really hot candles for $9.50. The gang at Shady Rest wanted Mona's 100th birthday party to be special, so they told Dan to spend the entire $100 and that's what he planned to do. How many of each type of candle did he need to buy to end up with exactly 100 candles and spend exactly $100?

OVERHEARD INFORMATION (PART I)

Read the story below, than turn the page and answer the questions.

> The detective overheard the jewelry thief tell his accomplice about the different places where he stashed the loot. He said, "The rubies are taped underneath the bathroom sink on the first floor. The pearls are in a box in the hall closet on the second floor. The emeralds are underneath the carpet in the den on the third floor. The opals are in a trunk in the attic."

OVERHEARD INFORMATION (PART II)

(Do not read this until you have read the previous page!)

The investigator overheard the information about where the stolen loot was stored, but didn't have anywhere to write it down! Answer the questions below to help her remember.

1. On which floor are the pearls found?

   _____

2. Which gems are found underneath the bathroom sink?

   _____

3. Where will you find the emeralds?

   _____

4. Which gems are found in a trunk?

   _____

Answers on page 174.

LIBRARY RETURNS

Joel and several friends went to the library after school to return some books. Each boy brought back one book. None of them checked out any other books from the library. Determine the name of each boy, the type of book that each returned, and what time each one returned the book (possible times were 3:30pm, 3:45pm, 4:00pm, and 4:15pm).

1. The 2 boys who returned books before 4:00pm, in no particular order, were Steve and the boy who returned the mystery book.

2. Mike returned his book 15 minutes after the humor book was returned.

3. The adventure book was returned at 4:15pm but not by Joel.

4. The science-fiction book was returned 15 minutes before Elliot's book.

5. The science-fiction book was returned by Mike.

Name	Type of Book	Time Returned

Answers on page 174.

CRYPTO-LOGIC

Each of the numbers in the sequence below represents a letter. Use the mathematical clues to determine which number stands for which letter and reveal the encrypted word.

Hint: Remember that a / indicates divided by, and that all sums in parentheses must be done first.

$$5\ 9\ 3\ 5\ 4\ 3\ 9\ 4\ 7$$

Clues:

$(P+1)$ squared$=O$

Fsquared$=\frac{1}{2}P$

Usquared$=N$

$(N+O)/T=T$

$S=O-P$

$U+R=S$

$P=2F$

$R+F=U$

ADDAGRAM

The detective found a list from the burglar and thinks it might indicate what the burglar plans to steal. But in addition to being scrambled, each word or phrase below is missing the same letter. Discover the missing letter, then unscramble the words. When you do, you'll find out what the burglar's targets are.

MAD NODS

A RAT

ADD ME

FINE RUG

Answers on page 174.

THINGS THAT SMELL GOOD (PART I)

Look at the crossword grid for 2 minutes. Then turn the page to see how many words you can remember.

```
G A R L I C        J         D
          A        A         O
P I N E T R E E S  S         U
          A        M         G
P E R F U M E      I     L   H
          E        N     I   N
C H O C O L A T E        C   U
    H     C        L     O   T
    O     O   O N I O N  S
F L O W E R S      N     R
    M     N     B A S I  L
    E             N      I
    W I N T E R G R E E  N
    I
    N
```

THINGS THAT SMELL GOOD (PART II)

(Do not read this until you have read the previous page!)

Check off the words you saw on the preceding page:

GARLIC ✓

LILAC

JASMINE ✓

ONIONS ✓

LAVENDER

CHOW MEIN ✓

LICORICE ✓

CARAMEL CORN ✓

DAISY

FORGET-ME-NOT

DOUGHNUTS ✓

PERIWINKLE

CHOCOLATE ✓

Answers on page 174.

DETECTIVE WORK!

Oh no! The museum has been raided and left a real mess! The detective has created a list of the museum's most valuable items. Can you find as many of these items as possible and discover which ones have been stolen?

Answers on page 175.

TREASURE HUNT

The treasure hunter visited eight cities, finding a clue in each one that led her to the treasure in the final city. Can you put the list of the eight cities she visited in order, using the information below?

The clue in Amsterdam led her immediately to the other city that began with an A.

She visited Skopje immediately before visiting Tokyo.

She did not find the treasure in Lima, Madrid, or Dodoma.

She visited the capital of Peru immediately after visiting the capital of Algeria.

Bangkok was one of the first three cities she visited.

The capital of Spain was the third city she visited.

She visited four other cities between her trips to Dodoma and Skopje.

Answers on page 175.

NICE PETS

In the Best Behaved Pet competition, the prize winners were about to be announced. Unfortunately, the judges have all their results wrongly recorded. Although each item is in the correct column, only 1 item in each column is correctly positioned.

1. The leopard is 2 places below Keith.

2. Arthur is 2 places above the crocodile.

3. Norma is 2 places above Evelyn.

4. Dennis is 3 places below Len.

5. The rhino is not in first place.

   Can you find the owner, pet, and pet name for each?

	Owner	Pet	Name
1	Arthur	cat	Keith
2	Bob	rhino	Len
3	Cathy	pig	Molly
4	Dennis	crocodile	Norma
5	Evelyn	leopard	Olive

Answers on page 175.

RBI PLAYERS

Five players on the same team had a phenomenal hitting run this past month. Their hitting has been pivotal to the team's current winning streak. All 5 had a significant increase in their batting averages and in their RBI totals. Determine the full name of each player (one first name was Mike and one last name was Case) and their current RBI stats.

1. Sam Waverly didn't have an RBI of 40.

2. Jack's RBI was 2 points higher than Mr. Templeton's and 2 points lower than Mr. Short's RBI.

3. The 2 players with RBIs in the 30s were Mr. Emerald and Clark.

4. Dan had the highest RBI of 44.

First Name	Last Name	Current RBI

	Case	Emerald	Short	Templeton	Waverly	36	38	40	42	44
Clark		X			X	X	X	O	O	X
Dan						X	X	X	O	O
Jack			X	X	X	X	X	O	X	X
Mike	X				X		X			X
Sam	X	X	X	X	O			X		X
36		X								
38		X								
40					X					
42										
44										

Answers on page 175.

SPY FLY

As an international spy, your mission is to travel from your headquarters at Seth Castle to your safe house at Faro. To disguise your trail, you must stop once—and only once—at each airport. See if you can find the cheapest route for your trip. Less than $280 would make you a Steady Sleuth; less than $260, a Cool Operator; less than $240, a Crafty Agent. If you can make it on $220, then you're a Super Spy!

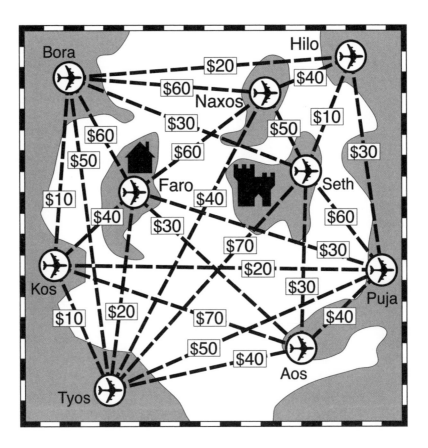

⊕ = Airport
♜ = Start
🏠 = Finish

Answers on page 175.

SHOE THROWING

At the annual Shoe Throwing contest, the list of prize winners has been compiled. However, due to a clerical error, the details have been mixed up. Although each last name, house name, and road is in the correct column, only one item in each column is correctly positioned. The following facts are certain about the correct order:

1. Fifth place is occupied by neither Potty Place nor Rut Road.

2. Carnegie is two places above Nirvana and three places above Nuts Close.

3. Neither Flop nor Dozy are fifth.

4. Potty Place is one place below Happy Heights and one place above Flop.

5. Neither Bedlam nor Whywurry are second.

6. Olive Crescent is one place below Bodman and three places above Dreary.

Can you give the correct name, house name, and road for each position?

	Name	House Name	Road
1	Arbuthnot	Whywurry	Menice Ave
2	Bodman	Happy Heights	Nuts Close
3	Carnegie	Claptrap	Olive Crescent
4	Dozy	Nirvana	Potty Place
5	Evertall	Bedlam	Quebec Street
6	Flop	Dreary	Rut Road

Answers on page 176.

CRYPTO-LOGIC

Each of the numbers in the sequence below represents a letter. Use the mathematical clues to determine which number stands for which letter and reveal the encrypted word.

Hint: Remember that a / indicates divided by, and that all sums in parentheses must be done first.

$$3 \ 2 \ 1 \ 9$$

Clues:

$X-E=M$ $\qquad$ $X-N=7$

$3N=E$ $\qquad$ $2M=A$

$X=10$

ADDAGRAM

The detective found a list that the burglar left behind. She knows that the burglar likes to scramble words, then remove one letter. To help the detective, discover the missing letter, then unscramble the words. When you do, you'll reveal the burglar's plans on a specific city and day, as well as his method of transport.

ERRED PUT

RIPS

DYED NEWS

ALPINE

Answers on page 176.

SPY FLY

As an international spy, your mission is to travel from your headquarters at Seth Castle to your safe house at Faro. To disguise your trail, you must stop once—and only once—at each airport. See if you can find the cheapest route for your trip. Less than $240 would make you a Steady Sleuth; less than $230, a Cool Operator; less than $220, a Crafty Agent. If you can make it on $210, then you're a Super Spy!

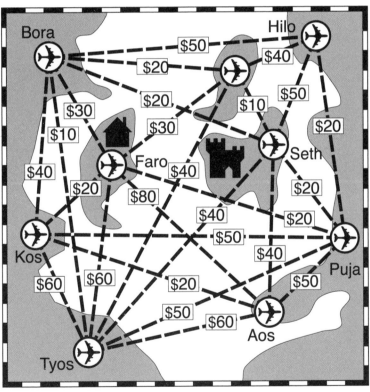

Answers on page 176.

GEMSTONE MATH

There are 6 types of gems. There is 1 gem of the first type, 2 of the second type, 3 of the third type, 4 of the fourth type, 5 of the fifth type, and 6 of the sixth type. From the information given below, can you tell how many gemstones there are of each kind?

There are at least 4 pearls. There are fewer than 3 zircons. There are more garnets than diamonds, but more sapphires than garnets. There are 2 more diamonds than aquamarines. There are fewer sapphires than pearls.

RICH RIDDLE

Hoping to avoid spending a lot of money on little Johnny's birthday present, Grandpa offered to give him in dollars the largest 2-digit number he could think of. What's the most money Johnny could have received from Grandpa for his birthday?

Answers on page 176.

ART FAIR STROLL

Can you determine the order of the booths at the art fair based on the information below?

You are walking past a line of booths at an art fair. You pass the booth with black and white photographs after you pass the place with oil portraits, but before you pass the place with color photographs. The place with quilts is immediately before the place that sells pottery. You pass the place with watercolors before you pass the places with color photography or with pottery. You pass at least 5 booths before you reach the places that sells decorative wind chimes. Immediately after you pass the place with the wind chimes, you pass the place that sells jewelry and the place that sells lamps, in that order. You pass the place with black and white photographs before you pass the place that sells wind chimes. There are exactly three booths between the place that sells the black and white photographs and the place that sells pottery.

REMEMBER ME?
(PART I)

Study this list of numbers and letters for 2 minutes then turn the page for a memory challenge.

8 4 D 2 T H 9 G T A 6 L

Answers on page 176.

REMEMBER ME?
(PART II)

(Do not read this until you have read the previous page!)

1. What is the only odd number that appears in the list?

2. What letter appears twice in the list?

3. What number appears between the letters H and G?

4. What is the last letter in the list?

5. What is the only letter that is not immediately preceded by or followed by a number?

WHAT'S FLIPPED IN VEGAS, STAYS IN VEGAS

Vivian loved Las Vegas. After seeing all the hottest shows, eating at all the hottest buffets, and walking down all the hottest sidewalks, Vivian was ready to try and get hot at gambling. Unfortunately, the only game she knew was flipping coins. Luckily, she found Caesar's Shack, a tiny casino that catered to coin flippers. The croupier—or in this case, flipier—invited her to play the house game. He would let her flip a coin 20 times. Each time the coin landed on heads, he would pay her $2. Each time the coin landed on tails, she had to pay him $3. Vivian was on edge but decided to give it a try. She flipped the coin 20 times and left Caesar's Shack with the same amount of money she came in with. How many times did the coin come up heads?

Answers on page 176.

AGE QUANDARY

In 12 year's time, the combined age of my 4 nieces will be 94.
What will it be in 5 year's time?

NUMBER NOGGIN-SCRATCHER (PART I)

Look at the list of numerals below for 1 minute, and then turn the page.

29751036497521639582

Answers on page 176.

NUMBER NOGGIN-SCRATCHER (PART II)

(Do not read this until you have read the previous page!)

Which one of the following groups of 3 numbers appears twice in the sequence?

A. 364 B. 975 C. 958 D. 649 E. 497

MAXIMS TO PONDER

Cryptograms are messages in substitution code. Break the code to read the message. For example, THE SMART CAT might become FVO QWGDF JGF if F is substituted for T, V for H, O for E, and so on. The code is the same for each of these cryptograms.

1. RHDKRQ FHJ QYHO TVC ZRHQRKQ
   WYP'C DRC QVLIRW MPCY SRC
   RPDMPRQ.

2. PRNRO HODVR ZMCX H QBYVQR ZXY
   MQ BHLIMPD JYVO BHOHLXVCR.

3. PRNRO FYYP H ZRORZYKE.

Answers on page 177.

MOVIE MANIA

A movie enthusiast plans to go to the cinema, but although he has decided on his list of preferences, he has copied them in his diary incorrectly. Although each item is in the correct column, only one item in each column is correctly positioned. The following facts are true about the correct order:

1. Screenz is not second.

2. Owen McAllen is one place above Olympic.

3. Neither Tim Panks nor Owen McAllen are first.

4. Screenz is one place below Gladys Hater.

5. Neither Lord Sings nor Gladys Hater are third.

Can you give the movie name, the cinema showing it, and the movie star for each position?

	Movie	Cinema	Star
1	Gladys Hater	Screenz	Ross Crawe
2	Forest Chump	Premiere	Tim Panks
3	Lord Sings	Worldwide	Owen McAllen
4	Atlantic 11	Olympic	Bud Pott

Answers on page 177.

PARADE PARKING

Even though signs were posted all over the city warning people not to park on certain streets because of the upcoming parade, the Polksville police department still towed 5 cars as a result of parking violations. Each of the 5 was picked up on a different street and at a different time, and each was a different brand of automobile. Using only the following clues, determine the brand and license plate for each car as well as when and where it was picked up.

1. The car picked up on Park Street was towed sometime after the Subaru.

2. The first car to be towed this morning was the Alfa Romeo.

3. Of the car that was illegally parked in Mitre Square and the one picked up at 6:15 am (which didn't have a license plate ending in P09), one was the Cadillac and the other had the license plate beginning with A14.

4. The car that was picked up on Bolero Court didn't have a Q in its plate.

5. The car picked up on Racine Boulevard didn't have a J in its license plate.

6. The Subaru was towed sometime after the Cadillac (which didn't have the license plate beginning with BYS).

7. Of the Hyundai and the car with the license plate ending in 01C, one was picked up at Park Street and the other at Bolero Court.

8. Neither the Isuzu, the car picked up on First Street (which was not the Isuzu), nor the car with the A14-S1D license plates were the first to be towed.

9. The last car to be towed did not have the A14-S1D license plates.

Answers on page 177.

Times	License Plates	Locations	Brands
6:10 A.M.			
6:15 A.M.			
6:20 A.M.			
6:25 A.M.			
6:30 A.M.			

		License Plates					Locations					Brands				
		A14-S1D	BYS-81S	JIB-P09	QE2-01C	XR6-192	Bolero Ct.	First St.	Mitre Sq.	Park St.	Racine Blvd.	Alfa Romeo	Cadillac	Hyundai	Isuzu	Subaru
Times	6:10 A.M.															
	6:15 A.M.															
	6:20 A.M.															
	6:25 A.M.															
	6:30 A.M.															
Brands	Alfa Romeo															
	Cadillac															
	Hyundai															
	Isuzu															
	Subaru															
Locations	Bolero Ct.															
	First Sq.															
	Mitre Sq.															
	Park St.															
	Racine Blvd.															

Answers on page 177.

CRYPTO-LOGIC

Each of the numbers in the sequence below represents a letter. Use the mathematical clues to determine which number stands for which letter and reveal the encrypted word.

Hint: Remember that a / indicates divided by, and that all sums in parentheses must be done first.

$$7\ 9\ 4\ 5\ 2$$

Clues: R=E+A   S=½U

E=2T   U=6

T=S-1   R-T=G

R=3S

TRY SAYING THIS
3 TIMES REALLY FAST

Which day of the week is 2 days before the day after the day 3 days after the day before Tuesday?

Answers on page 177.

GLOBE QUEST

Fly from Miami to Seattle, visiting each city once. See if you can find the cheapest route for your trip. Less than $356 would make you a Super Vacationer; less than $343, a Passport Pioneer; less than $330, a Seasoned Traveler. If you can make the trip for $298, then you're a Globe Quester!

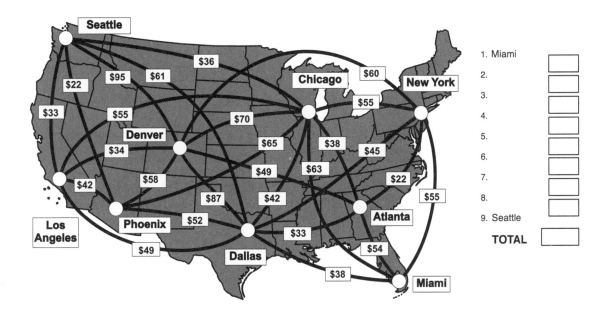

1. Miami
2.
3.
4.
5.
6.
7.
8.
9. Seattle
TOTAL

Answers on page 177.

RACE TO THE TRUTH

Can you determine the order of the 7 runners in the race based on the information below?

John placed immediately ahead of Morgan. Tasha didn't win the race but was one of the top 3 runners. Benedict was ahead of John, but there was one other runner between them. Kelsey was either 4th or 7th. Laura was one of the last 3 runners. Jess came in behind Morgan, but there was at least one runner between them.

A BRIGHT IDEA

A billionaire offered three men this challenge: "The man who can fill this room with something using the least amount of money will win a million dollars." The first man spent $100 and filled the room with lots of air-filled balloons. The second man spent $10 and filled the room with a single, giant air-filled balloon. The third man spent nothing and won the million dollars. What did he do?

Answers on page 178.

VISUALIZE THIS!

I am walking down a road filled with many landmarks. After crossing a bridge, I must climb over a fence but not before I cross the aqueduct. The restaurant I pass is farther than the signpost before the bridge, with 5 other landmarks in between. The signpost lies at the bottom of a great hill, and the bridge is located immediately after the signpost. The final landmark is not the canal lock, and it isn't between the signpost and the restaurant. The wishing well and the scarecrow are the last 2 landmarks before the restaurant. The traffic lights are not found near the beginning of the list and have but one landmark adjacent to them. The other 2 landmarks in question are a ditch and a crossroads, the latter of which does not begin the list but is located before the hill. In what order do I encounter these landmarks on my journey?

STOPPING FOR DIRECTIONS (PART I)

Study the arrows below for 20 seconds before turning to the next page for a memory challenge...

Answers on page 178.

STOPPING FOR DIRECTIONS (PART II)

(Do not read this until you have read the previous page!)

Can you identify the correct order of the arrows from the previous page?

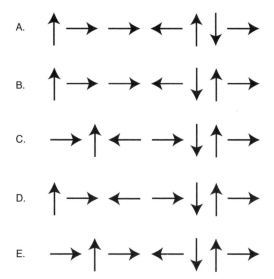

A. ↑ → → ← ↑↓ →

B. ↑ → → ← ↓↑ →

C. → ↑ ← → ↓↑ →

D. ↑ → ← → ↓↑ →

E. → ↑ → ← ↓↑ →

APPLE ORDER

A market trader received a consignment of apples and found that, to his chagrin, several were rotten. He counted them and found that 176 were rotten, which was 32 percent of the consignment.

How many apples were in the consignment?

Answers on page 178.

GLOBE QUEST

Fly from Miami to Seattle, visiting each city on this map once. See if you can find the cheapest route for your trip. Less than $437 would make you a Super Vacationer; less than $430, a Passport Pioneer; less than $390, a Seasoned Traveler. If you can make the trip for $369, then you're a Globe Quester!

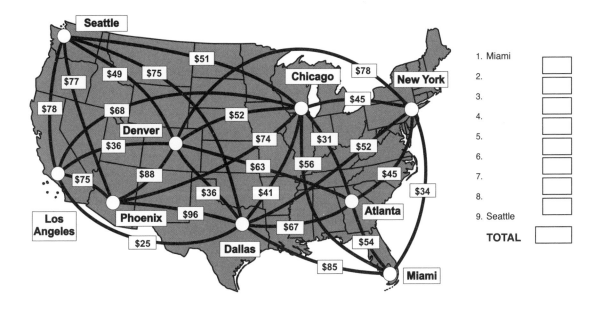

1. Miami
2.
3.
4.
5.
6.
7.
8.
9. Seattle

TOTAL

Answers on page 178.

TOP SCORERS

The Newcastle Junior Hockey League is offering a $1,000 scholarship this year to the player who scores the most goals. The season is still far from over, but the competition is getting fierce! Using the clues below, determine the name of each of the current top-5 goal-scoring players, which team they play for, what town they're from, and how many goals they've scored.

1. Greg Greyson isn't from Vesuvius.

2. Dale Dakota has scored one less goal so far than the Giants player.

3. Between Greg Greyson and the Giants player, one has the highest number of total goals so far and the other is from Madridge.

4. Sean Stang is from either Playalinda or Madridge.

5. Either Dale Dakota or the player with exactly 24 goals scored is from Smallville.

6. The 5 players are Dale Dakota, Greg Greyson, the Mustangs player, the one with the second-highest number of goals, and the one from Smallville.

7. Neither the Fighters player nor the Giants player has exactly 24 goals scored this season.

8. Either Peter Paris or Greg Greyson is from Madridge.

9. The player who currently has the highest number of goals doesn't play for either the Fighters or the Cowboys.

Goals Scored	Player	Team	Town
23			
24			
25			
26			
27			

		Player					Team					Town				
		Dale Dakota	Grey Greyson	Lou Lilla	Peter Paris	Sean Stang	Cowboys	Fighters	Giants	Mustangs	Polar Bears	Harley	Madridge	Playalinda	Smallville	Vesuvius
Goals Scored	23															
	24															
	25															
	26															
	27															
Town	Harley															
	Madridge															
	Playalinda															
	Smallville															
	Vesuvius															
Team	Cowboys															
	Fighters															
	Giants															
	Mustangs															
	Polar Bears															

Answers on page 178.

GEMSTONE MATH

There are 6 types of gems. There is 1 gem of the first type, 2 of the second type, 3 of the third type, 4 of the fourth type, 5 of the fifth type, and 6 of the sixth type. From the information given below, can you tell how many gemstones there are of each kind?

There are 3 times more pearls than peridots. There are 2 more agates than there are garnets. There are 3 more pieces of turquoise than there are rubies. There are more agates than pearls.

FILL 'ER UP

You need to measure 6 gallons of water, but you only have a 9-gallon bucket (bucket A) and a 4-gallon bucket (bucket B). How do you do this? There is an unlimited water supply, and both buckets start empty.

Answers on page 178.

SPY FLY

As an international spy, your mission is to travel from your headquarters at Seth Castle to your safe house at Faro. To disguise your trail, you must stop once—and only once—at each airport. See if you can find the cheapest route for your trip. Less than $290 would make you a Steady Sleuth; less than $280, a Cool Operator; less than $270, a Crafty Agent. If you can make it on $250, then you're a Super Spy!

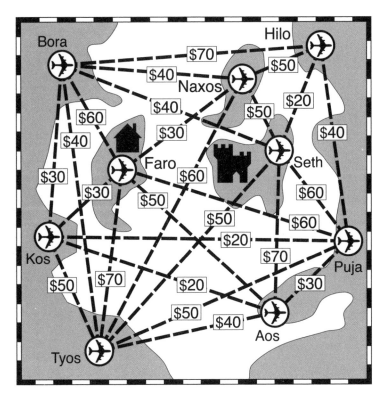

 = Airport

= Start

= Finish

Answers on page 179.

CRYPTO-LOGIC

Each of the numbers in the sequence below represents a letter. Use the mathematical clues to determine which number stands for which letter and reveal the encrypted word.

Hint: Remember that a / indicates divided by, and that all sums in parentheses must be done first.

5723

Clues: | L = 10 | S = 1 |
| L / N = D | D + 2 = O |
| D – 4 = S | L – O = E |

SEQUENCE

What comes next?

Adam's rib, Camp David, ease off, _____

Gas stations, go Dutch, jam sessions, Baton Rouge, Miami Beach

Answers on page 179.

NAME THAT NAME (PART I)

Carefully study the names and occupations below for 5 minutes before turning the page. But beware—some of these names can be misleading...

Tony Sparrow	Entertainer
Samuel Painter	Carpenter
Frank Cook	Chauffeur
Samantha Kitchen	Tailor
Alan Wood	Baker
Annette Driver	Cook
Julia Singer	Ornithologist

NAME THAT NAME (PART II)

(Do not read this until you have read the previous page!)

Can you complete the table with the correct surnames and professions?

Surnames: Wood, Singer, Painter, Cook, Driver, Kitchen, and Sparrow

Professions: Ornithologist, entertainer, tailor, baker, chauffeur, cook, and carpenter.

First Name	Surname	Profession
Tony	Sparrow	
Samuel		Carpenter
Frank	Cook	
Samantha		Tailor
Alan		
Annette		Cook
Julia	Singer	

Answers on page 179.

GLOBE QUEST

Fly from Miami to Seattle, visiting each city on this map once. See if you can find the cheapest route for your trip. Less than $410 would make you a Super Vacationer; less than $390, a Passport Pioneer; less than $370, a Seasoned Traveler. If you can make the trip for $314, then you're a Globe Quester!

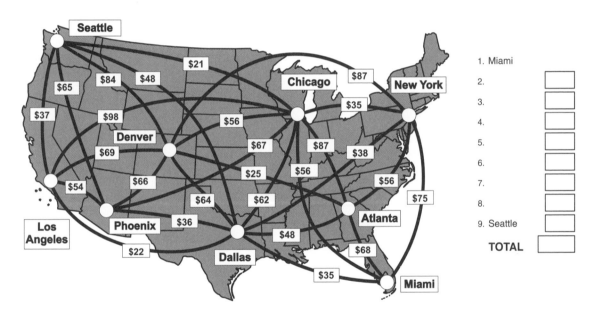

1. Miami
2. ☐
3. ☐
4. ☐
5. ☐
6. ☐
7. ☐
8. ☐
9. Seattle ☐
TOTAL ☐

Answers on page 179.

HOCKEY CARDS

Five avid card collectors attended last Saturday's annual Sports Collectibles Convention in Pasadena. Each rushed immediately to the hockey-card tables, where they pored over hundreds of rare and collectible cards available for purchase. By the end of the day, each collector had purchased a single rare hockey card—each sold for a different price and featured a different hockey player from a different season. Using the clues below, determine which player's card each collector purchased, as well as the year and price of each card.

1. The Herbie Hillstrand card cost $58.

2. Between Keaton and Eddie, one bought the Hank Harris card and the other bought a card that was originally printed in 1994.

3. Abe didn't buy the 1986 card.

4. The Chucky Colburn card (which wasn't the most expensive of the 5 cards) was not printed in 1989.

5. Reid's card cost him $9 more than what Jesse paid for his card.

6. The 1993 card (which didn't feature Hank Harris) didn't cost $67.

7. Keaton's card came out sometime before 1993.

8. The 1989 card cost $9 less than Reid's card.

9. Between the card Keaton purchased and the Herbie Hillstrand card, one was the cheapest of the 5 cards and the other was printed in 1986.

10. The $49 card featured either Hubert Hansen or Chucky Colburn.

11. Between Reid and the person who bought the Harris card, one bought the Hillstrand card and the other paid $40.

Price	Collector	Player	Year
$40			
$49			
$58			
$67			
$76			

		Collector					Player					Year				
		Abe	Eddie	Jesse	Keaton	Reid	Colburn	Fourtner	Hansen	Harris	Hillstrand	1983	1986	1989	1993	1994
Price	$40															
	$49															
	$58															
	$67															
	$76															
Year	1983															
	1986															
	1989															
	1993															
	1994															
Player	Colburn															
	Fourtner															
	Hansen															
	Harris															
	Hillstrand															

Answers on page 179.

MEND THE BRIDGES

Rain has swept through the entire county, flooding all the bridges indicated by circles. Your job is to travel to each location—A through I, in any order—by restoring only 2 of the bridges.

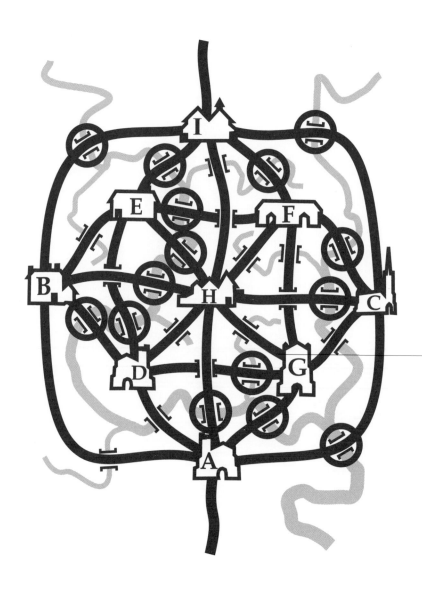

Answers on page 179.

SPY FLY

As an international spy, your mission is to travel from your headquarters at Seth Castle to your safe house at Faro. To disguise your trail, you must stop once—and only once—at each airport. See if you can find the cheapest route for your trip. Less than $320 would make you a Steady Sleuth; less than $310, a Cool Operator; less than $300, a Crafty Agent. If you can make it on $260, then you're a Super Spy!

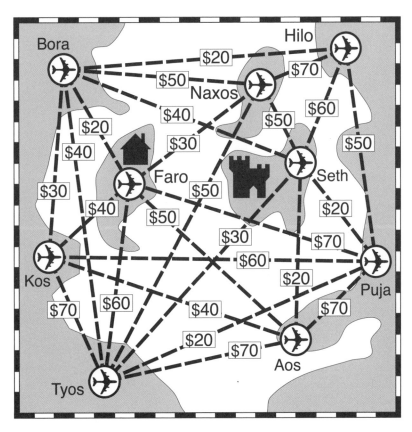

✈ = Airport
♖ = Start
🏠 = Finish

Answers on page 180.

PUBLISHING POETRY

Palindrome Press has 5 new poetry books coming out this year, and they've had to bring on several new editors to ensure that each book makes its intended launch date. Each book has a different author, and each has been assigned to a different editor to get the manuscript ready for publication. Using only the clues below, match each book to its author and editor, and determine the month in which each book is scheduled to be published.

1. Valerie isn't the editor assigned to Fanny Farnsworth's new book (which isn't titled *My Own Mamon*).

2. Of *For Gerald* and *Driven Away*, one was written by Betty Beaufort and the other is scheduled for a September launch.

3. Among *Nine Takes* and the book Jeff is editing, one will be released in November and the other was written by Dorothy Dickens.

4. Of *My Own Mamon* and the newest book by Penny Penington, one will be the last of the five to be published and the other has been assigned to Marilyn for editing.

5. The book Timothy is editing will be released one month after *Driven Away*.

6. *California* (which isn't being edited by Marilyn) will be launched sometime before *My Own Mamon* and sometime after *August*.

7. For *Gerald* (which wasn't written by Ms. Beaufort) will be released some time before the book that Timothy is editing.

Months	Authors	Titles	Editors
August			
September			
October			
November			
December			

		Authors					Titles					Editors				
		Beaufort	Dickens	Farnsworth	Leary	Pennington	California	Driven Away	For Gerald	Thieves City	Nine Takes	Jeff	Lyn	Marilyn	Timothy	Valerie
Months	August															
	September															
	October															
	November															
	December															
Editors	Jeff															
	Lyn															
	Marilyn															
	Timothy															
	Valerie															
Titles	California															
	Driven Away															
	For Gerald															
	Thieves City															
	Nine Takes															

Answers on page 180.

CRYPTO-LOGIC

Each of the numbers in the sequence below represents a letter. Use the mathematical clues to determine which number stands for which letter and reveal the encrypted word.

Hint: Remember that a / indicates divided by, and that all sums in parentheses must be done first.

72406

Clues: $S = 5$ $U - S + 1 = C$ $G / 2 = A$

$M + S = 12$ $C / 2 = E$ $C - (A + G) = I$

$2S = U$ $E + 1 = G$

ROBBER RIDDLE

Cryptograms are messages in substitution code. Break the code to read the riddle and its answer. For example, THE SMART CAT might become FVO QWGDF JGF if F is substituted for T, V for H, O for E, and so on.

DSB WRW GSV ILYYVI DVZI DSRGV TOLEVH?

SV WRWM'T DZMG GL YV XZFTSG IVW-SZMWVW.

Answers on page 180.

SPY FLY

As an international spy, your mission is to travel from your headquarters at Seth Castle to your safe house at Faro. To disguise your trail, you must stop once—and only once—at each airport. See if you can find the cheapest route for your trip. Less than $290 would make you a Steady Sleuth; less than $280, a Cool Operator; less than $270, a Crafty Agent. If you can make it on $260, then you're a Super Spy!

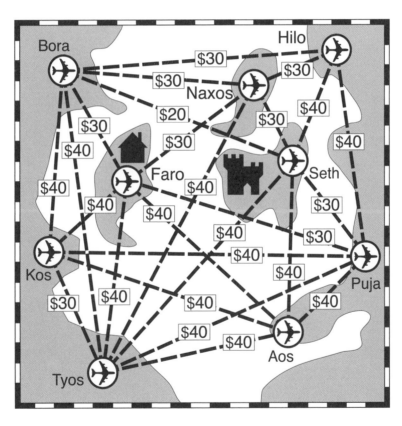

= Airport
= Start
= Finish

Answers on page 180.

VISUALIZE THIS!

Can you determine the order in which the toys appear based on the information below?

I am walking through my house, picking up my child's toys, which are scattered all over the place. I do not pick up the Lego after the catapult, but I do pick it up directly after the abacus. The action man is the only item I pick up in between the first 2 toys mentioned in this passage. Before these toys I've mentioned, I pick up 3 items, the middle one of which is a toy ball. All the others are picked up by me after the catapult, and the xylophone is neither last to be retrieved, nor first out of these. Out of these 5, the coloring book is picked up before the xylophone, as are 2 other toys—both of which are placed after the coloring book. The toy boat, while one of the 5, is not one of these 2. The latter of these 2 is a teddy bear, and the former is a racing car. The first toy to be picked up is not a keyboard. And the toy I haven't mentioned that I did pick up was a toy truck.

Answers on page 180.

WHAT COMES NEXT?

Study the series of letters below. Every letter in each series is the first letter of a word, and all the words in each series are related. For example, if the first 4 letters of a series were M, V, E, M, they would stand for Mercury, Venus, Earth, and Mars. Logically, the next letter would be J, for Jupiter.

Continue each series below by discovering the next logical word.

1. H, H, L, B, B, C, N, ___

2. K, P, C, O, F, G, ___

3. P, E, M, D, A, ___

NUMBER NOGGIN-SCRATCHER (PART I)

Look at the list of numerals below for 1 minute, and then turn the page.

543209879099554

Answers on page 180.

NUMBER NOGGIN-SCRATCHER (PART II)

(Do not read this until you have read the previous page!)

Which one of the following groups of 3 numbers ended the sequence on the previous page?

A. 543 B. 098 C. 954 D. 554 E. 544

LOTTERY LOGIC

Gary, Hurley, and Joe pool their money every week to play the lottery. Gary puts in $3, Hurley puts in $2, Joe puts in $1. With this money, they buy six tickets. Because they put in different amounts—and because Joe doesn't appear to be too bright—they decide to divide any winnings the following way: Gary would get one-half, Hurley would get one-third, and Joe would get one-ninth. The friends finally get a winner, and the prize is $34. The prize was paid in dollar bills, and none of them had any coins to make change. Gary and Hurley couldn't figure out how to divide the dollar bills in the pot. Joe reached into his pocket, pulled something out, and the friends were able to divide their winnings according to the agreed-upon deal. What did Joe pull out of his pocket?

Answers on page 181.

DOGGIE DINNERS

One bag of dog food can feed 8 puppies or 6 dogs. If you have 8 bags of the same dog food and need to feed 20 puppies, how many dogs can you also feed?

A. 24

B. 30

C. 33

D. 40

E. 53

COURIER CONFUSION (PART I)

Mr. Sawyer has a letter to deliver but can't remember all the details. Study the fictitious address below for 2 minutes and then turn the page to help him fill in the blanks.

Don Jensen

The Willows

4th Floor

94 Grand Oaks Avenue

Bakersfield,

CA 93301

Answers on page 181.

COURIER CONFUSION (PART II)

(Do not read this until you have read the previous page!)

Help Mr. Sawyer by filling in the missing information.

> Don _____
>
> The _____
>
> _____th Floor
>
> 94 _____ Oaks _____
>
> Bakersfield,
>
> CA _____

RIDDLE

Bernard died in Texas, while Colin died at sea. Why was Colin's death a cause for much relief?

Answers on page 181.

ANSWER IN THE ROUND

What has four legs, a head, and leaves? To find the answer to this riddle, look at the words in the circles below. Cross off all the words that appear in all three circles. The words that are left will be the answer.

double rude
daydream decorate
tree rush term
tangle range remove
trash railroad
deal dining thief recess
diary thoughtful
root

root room
thoughtful decorate
rush tree diary
trash
tangle railroad remove
range recess
rude thief
deal
term daydream
double

diary rude
trash rush railroad
tree range deal
daydream decorate tangle
remove table recess
term double root thief
thoughtful

Answers on page 181.

MEND THE BRIDGES

Rain has swept through the entire county, flooding all the bridges indicated by circles. Your job is to travel to each location—A through I, in any order—by restoring only 2 of the bridges.

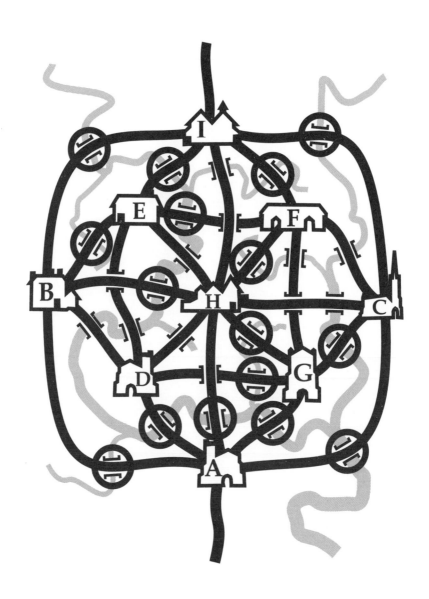

Answers on page 181.

SPY FLY

As an international spy, your mission is to travel from your headquarters at Seth Castle to your safe house at Faro. To disguise your trail, you must stop once—and only once—at each airport. See if you can find the cheapest route for your trip. Less than $290 would make you a Steady Sleuth; less than $280, a Cool Operator; less than $270, a Crafty Agent. If you can make it on $260, then you're a Super Spy!

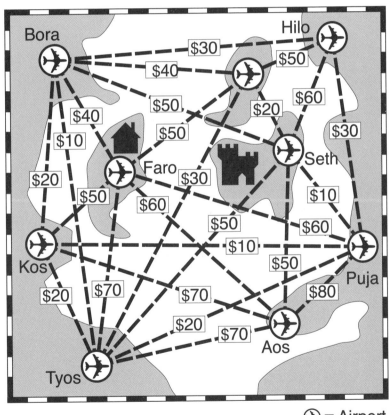

= Airport
= Start
= Finish

Answers on page 182.

CRYPTO-LOGIC

Each of the numbers in the sequence below represents a letter. Use the mathematical clues to determine which number stands for which letter and reveal the encrypted word.

Hint: Remember that a / indicates divided by, and that all sums in parentheses must be done first.

$$5\ 6\ 9\ 4\ 3\ 6\ 1\ 2$$

Clues:

I repeats	U / ½ I = P	½ Y = F
I - 1 = S	½ P = Y	D + F = M
2I = U	2 x Y squared = D	P - F = L

RACE TO THE TRUTH

Can you determine the order of the 7 runners in the race based on the information below?

Tina was either the winner of the race or the person who placed last. Michaela was not in the top three, but neither did she place last. There were 2 runners between Lawrence and Salman, who placed somewhere ahead of Genevieve. Kendra didn't beat out Lawrence, but she was ahead of Michaela. There was one runner behind Michaela but before Dirk.

Answers on page 182.

GEMSTONE MATH

There are 6 types of gems. There is 1 gem of the first type, 2 of the second type, 3 of the third type, 4 of the fourth type, 5 of the fifth type, and 6 of the sixth type. From the information given below, can you tell how many gemstones there are of each kind?

There is more than 1 amethyst, and more than 3 garnets. There are twice as many amethysts as there are pieces of jade. There are twice as many sapphires as there are rubies. There is an even number of pieces of topaz. There are more sapphires than amethysts.

MIXED FIGURES (PART I)

Study the figures below for 1 minute, and then turn the page for a memory challenge...

♪ ▶ 5 $ 4 Ω 8 ♠ 9 ▶ W 5 □

Answers on page 182.

MIXED FIGURES
(PART II)

(Do not read this until you have read the previous page!)

1. Which symbol appears twice?

2. Which number appears twice?

WORD COLUMNS

Find the hidden quote from Samuel Johnson by using the letters directly below each of the blank squares. Each letter is used once. A black square indicates the end of a word.

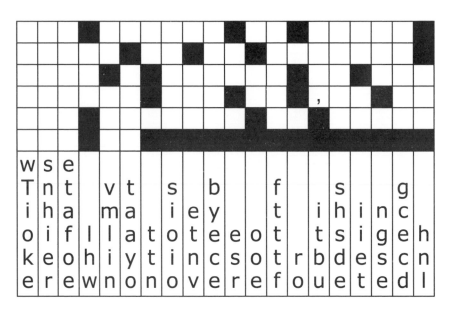

Answers on page 182.

SPY FLY

As an international spy, your mission is to travel from your headquarters at Seth Castle to your safe house at Faro. To disguise your trail, you must stop once—and only once—at each airport. See if you can find the cheapest route for your trip. Less than $290 would make you a Steady Sleuth; less than $280, a Cool Operator; less than $270, a Crafty Agent. If you can make it on $250, then you're a Super Spy!

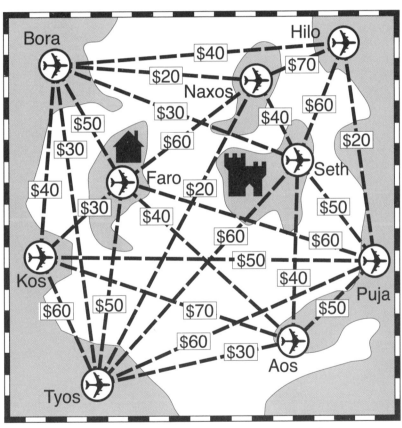

Answers on page 182.

APPLETON ARENA

The Appleton Arena is supposed to host 5 hockey games this week, but Frank Ferrymore, the scheduling coordinator, came down with a bad case of the flu, and no one is sure which teams are playing and when! Using the clues below, help make sense of the schedule by determining which teams are playing each other on which days and at which times.

1. The 2:30 P.M. game is scheduled to take place one day before the Sharks game.

2. The 2:45 P.M. game won't include the Camelbacks and won't be on Thursday.

3. The 1:45 P.M. game will feature the Marlins.

4. Between Wednesday's game and the 2:45 P.M. game, one will feature the Camelbacks and the other the Skaters.

5. The 5 games are the Sharks game, the Penguins game, the Anglers game, the one that starts at 2:45 P.M., and the last game of the week (which won't start before noon).

6. The only game this week that starts in the morning won't feature the Raiders.

7. The 4:00 P.M. game will take place the day before the 2:45 P.M. game.

8. The Bluebirds won't play on Friday.

Day Of The Week	Home Team	Away Team	Game Time
Monday			
Tuesday			
Wednesday			
Thursday			
Friday			

		Home Team					Away Team					Game Time				
		Anglers	Bluebirds	Camelbacks	Drafters	Sharks	Marlins	Penguins	Raiders	Skaters	Twins	11:00 A.M.	1:45 P.M.	2:30 P.M.	2:45 P.M.	4:00 P.M.
Day Of The Week	Monday															
	Tuesday															
	Wednesday															
	Thursday															
	Friday															
Game Time	11:00 A.M.															
	1:45 P.M.															
	2:30 P.M.															
	2:45 P.M.															
	4:00 P.M.															
Away Team	Marlins															
	Penguins															
	Raiders															
	Skaters															
	Twins															

Answers on page 183.

NAME CALLING

Decipher the encoded word in the quip below using the numbers and letters on the phone pad. Remember that each number can stand for 3 or 4 possible letters.

2-2-8-4-2-7 Emptor — Beware of the fish!

NAME CALLING

Decipher the encoded words in the proverb below using the numbers and letters on the phone pad. Remember that each number can stand for 3 or 4 possible letters.

When the house is 7–9–3–7–8, 3–8–3–7–9–8–4–4–6–4 turns up.

Answers on page 183.

EAT YOUR VEGGIES (PART I)

Study these items for a minute, ignoring the caption, then turn the page for a memory challenge.

Tomatoes	Beets
Peas	Spinach
Sweet potato	Pumpkins
Radishes	Parsley

EAT YOUR VEGGIES (PART II)

Do not look at this until you have read the previous page!

Check off the vegetables seen on the previous page.

CELERY	BELL PEPPERS
CORN	BROCCOLI
ONIONS	OKRA
TURNIP	ENDIVE
SQUASH	MUSHROOMS
POTATOES	GARLIC
LIMA BEANS	

RACE TO THE TRUTH

Can you determine the order of the 7 runners in the race based on the information below?

Patrice was in neither the top two slots in the race or the bottom two. Jonathan just beat out Courtney to come in directly behind Tony. Two other runners were behind Jonathan but before Rob. Kenneth beat out Cameron, but not Patrice.

Answers on page 183.

SPY FLY

As an international spy, your mission is to travel from your headquarters at Seth Castle to your safe house at Faro. To disguise your trail, you must stop once—and only once—at each airport. See if you can find the cheapest route for your trip. Less than $280 would make you a Steady Sleuth; less than $270, a Cool Operator; less than $250, a Crafty Agent. If you can make it on $230, then you're a Super Spy!

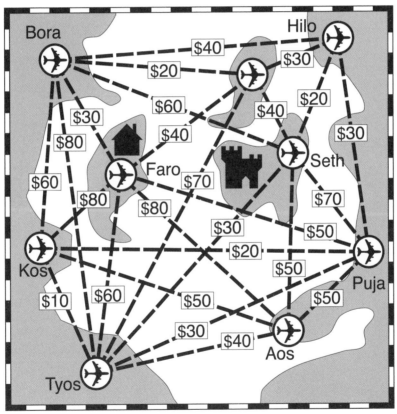

= Airport
= Start
= Finish

Answers on page 183.

CRYPTO-LOGIC

Each of the numbers in the sequence below represents a letter. Use the mathematical clues to determine which number stands for which letter and reveal the encrypted word.

Hint: Remember that a / indicates divided by, and that all sums in parentheses must be done first.

$$1\ 5\ 3\ 9\ 8\ 2\ 5\ 6$$

Clues:

R repeats	$E \times R = S$	$3 \times (\frac{1}{2}Y) = C$
$R - (R - 1) = T$	$S + E = L$	$(C-R) \times 2 = K$
$2T = E$	$L / 2 = Y$	$\frac{1}{2}K - T = I$

GEMSTONE MATH

There are 6 types of gems. There is 1 gem of the first type, 2 of the second type, 3 of the third type, 4 of the fourth type, 5 of the fifth type, and 6 of the sixth type. From the information given below, can you tell how many gemstones there are of each kind?

There is an even number of pearls and an odd number of sapphires. There are 2 more pieces of topaz than there are of jade. There are fewer pieces of turquoise than there are rubies or sapphires. There are 2 more rubies than there are pearls. There is 1 more piece of turquoise than there is of jade.

Answers on page 183.

GLOBE QUEST

Fly from Miami to Seattle, visiting each city once. See if you can find the cheapest route for your trip. Less than $410 would make you a Super Vacationer; less than $390, a Passport Pioneer; less than $370, a Seasoned Traveler. If you can make the trip for $326, then you're a Globe Quester!

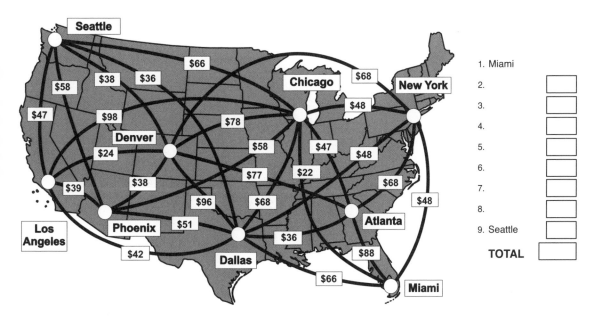

1. Miami
2. [ ]
3. [ ]
4. [ ]
5. [ ]
6. [ ]
7. [ ]
8. [ ]
9. Seattle [ ]
TOTAL [ ]

Answers on page 183.

STOCK MARKET GAINS

It was a banner day at the local investment club, where every single member made a profit on their investments! One of the club rules is that each member must own only 1 stock, and no 2 members can own the same stock. Using the following clues, determine the symbol and current price of the stock owned by each investor, as well as the percentage each stock's price increased today:

1. The least-expensive stock (which didn't go up today by either 2.6% or 5.1%) is owned by either Richard or Pablo.

2. Of Pablo's stock and the stock priced at $8.22 per share, one has the symbol DZZW and the other went up in value 1.9% today.

3. The stock that gained 2.0% today is priced 7 cents less than CPYL, which has a higher per-share price than Carl's stock.

4. Richard's stock is either TTHP or the stock that gained 1.9% in today's market.

5. The stock with the highest price didn't have the smallest percentage gain today.

6. AMDQ is priced 7 cents less than the stock Pablo owns.

7. Izzy's stock (which isn't MLVX) gained more than 1.2% in today's trading.

8. The second-most-expensive stock didn't go up by either 2.0% or 5.1%.

9. The stock that gained 2.0% today is priced 7 cents higher than the stock that gained 1.9%.

Stock Prices	Symbols	Investors	Increases
$8.15			
$8.22			
$8.29			
$8.36			
$8.43			

		Symbols					Investors					Increases				
		AMDQ	CPYL	DZZW	MLVX	TTHP	Carl	Izzy	Pablo	Ralph	Richard	+1.2%	+1.9%	+2.0%	+2.6%	+5.1%
Stock Prices	$8.15															
	$8.22															
	$8.29															
	$8.36															
	$8.43															
Increases	+1.2%															
	+1.9%															
	+2.0%															
	+2.6%															
	+5.1%															
Investors	Carl															
	Izzy															
	Pablo															
	Ralph															
	Richard															

Answers on page 184.

ROOK JUMPING

Make a series of jumps from start to finish, moving like a rook chess piece (up, down, sideways, but not diagonally). The number in the corner of each cell indicates the distance of each jump. Write the sequence of your jumps in the cells (1, 2, 3, etc.).

4	4	2	0 FINISH	4	3 START
2	4	4	4	1	4
1	5	1	3	4	1
5	3	2	3	3	5
2	4	5	5	2	2
2	3	4	2	4	5

Answers on page 184.

LIAR'S LOGIC!

Use the following information to figure out who is lying and who is telling the truth. There are 2 truth tellers and 2 liars. You know that A is telling the truth.

Person A says person C is lying.

Person B says person D is lying.

Person C says person B is telling the truth.

Person D says person A is telling the truth.

NUMBER JUMBLE (PART I)

Study the numbers below for 2 minutes before turning the page for a memory challenge.

397165

426193

659327

867154

Answers on page 184.

NUMBER JUMBLE (PART II)

(Do not read this until you have read the previous page!)

1. What is the only number that appears in every row?

2. What number appears three times down the fourth column?

3. What number appears twice down the third column?

4. What number appears at the end of the first row?

MEND THE BRIDGES

Rain has swept through the entire county, flooding all the bridges indicated by circles. Your job is to travel to each location—A through I, in any order—by restoring only 2 of the bridges.

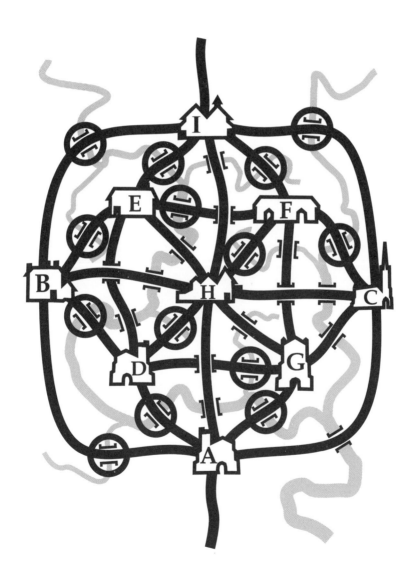

Answers on page 184.

GLOBE QUEST

Fly from Miami to Seattle, visiting each city once. See if you can find the cheapest route for your trip. Less than $435 would make you a Super Vacationer; less than $425, a Passport Pioneer; less than $400, a Seasoned Traveler. If you can make the trip for $364, then you're a Globe Quester!

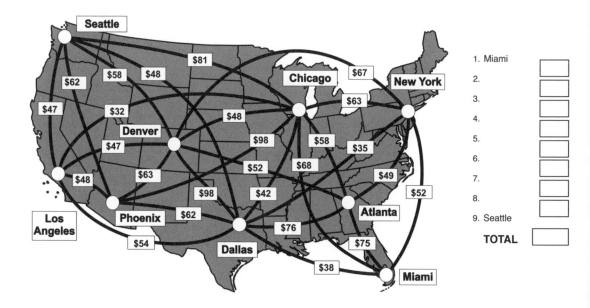

1. Miami

2.

3.

4.

5.

6.

7.

8.

9. Seattle

TOTAL

Answers on page 184.

OVERHEARD INFORMATION (PART I)

Read the story below, than turn the page and answer the questions.

The detective overheard the jewelry thief tell her accomplice about the different places where she stashed the loot. She said, "The emeralds are underneath the loose floorboard in the house in Paris. The diamonds are behind the false brick wall in the basement of the house in Prague. The rubies are stored in a safe in the spare bedroom of the apartment in Budapest. The opals are hidden in a trunk in the attic of the chalet in Switzerland. The strings of pearls are taped to the underside of the desk drawer in the den of the house in Luxembourg."

OVERHEARD INFORMATION (PART II)

(Do not read this until you have read the previous page!)

The investigator overheard the information about where the stolen loot was stored, but didn't have anywhere to write it down! Answer the questions below to help him remember.

1. The rubies can be found in a house in Prague.
    A. True
    B. False

2. The strings of pearls are taped to the underside of the desk drawer in the den of the apartment in Luxembourg.
    A. True
    B. False

3. The emeralds are found underneath a floorboard in Paris.
    A. True
    B. False

4. The diamonds are found behind a false brick wall.
    A. True
    B. False

5. The opals are found in Budapest
    A. True
    B. False

Answers on page 185.

SPY FLY

As an international spy, your mission is to travel from your headquarters at Seth Castle to your safe house at Faro. To disguise your trail, you must stop once—and only once—at each airport. See if you can find the cheapest route for your trip. Less than $260 would make you a Steady Sleuth; less than $250, a Cool Operator; less than $240, a Crafty Agent. If you can make it on $230, then you're a Super Spy!

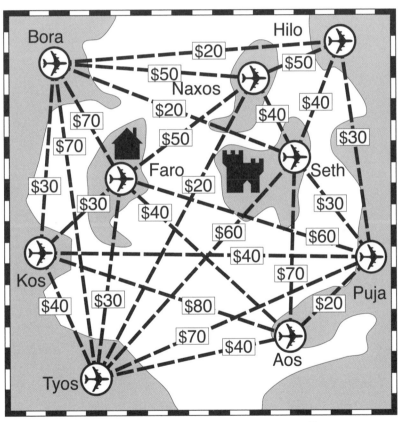

Answers on page 185.

CRYPTO-LOGIC

Each of the numbers in the sequence below represents a letter. Use the mathematical clues to determine which number stands for which letter and reveal the encrypted word.

Hint: Remember that a / indicates divided by, and that all sums in parentheses must be done first.

$$5\ 9\ 1\ 3\ 7\ 3\ 2$$

Clues:
- E repeats
- W<R<E
- O=H+S
- O>H>S
- R squared+1=H
- O-3=T
- T+1=V

ROBBER RIDDLE

Cryptograms are messages in substitution code. Break the code to read the riddle and its answer. For example, THE SMART CAT might become FVO QWGDF JGF if F is substituted for T, V for H, O for E, and so on.

BWD NXN IWO LJGVQKG TUOS WXH

HKMZ BWOS XI HIKGION IT GKXS?

WO BKH WTUXSV PTG HTRO MWKSVO XS
IWO BOKIWOG.

Answers on page 185.

VISUALIZE THIS!

On my staircase are many items of clothing. My red sock is above my pants and just below my tie. My right gym shoe is above my tie and immediately below my cowboy hat. My blue sock is below my jacket, which is just below my belt. My jacket is below my white shirt. My white shirt is below my winter coat but immediately below my left gym shoe, which is above my right gym shoe, and also above my cowboy hat. My boxer shorts are lying almost at the top of the stairs, just below my waistcoat. My belt is just below my pants. If I walk up the stairs from the bottom to the top picking up the items, in what order will I collect them?

ARROWS (PART I)

Study the image below for 10 seconds, then wait one minute before turning the page for a memory challenge.

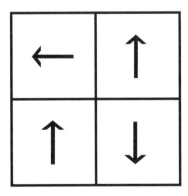

Answers on page 185.

ARROWS (PART II)

Do not read this until you have read the previous page!

Which one of the following groupings did you see on the previous page?

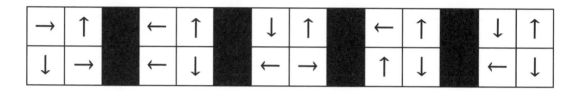

GEMSTONE MATH

There are 7 types of gems. There is 1 gem of the first type, 2 of the second type, 3 of the third type, 4 of the fourth type, 5 of the fifth type, 6 of the sixth type, and 7 of the seventh type. From the information given below, can you tell how many gemstones there are of each kind?

There are at least 5 garnets. There are fewer than 4 rubies. There are 2 more amethysts than rubies. There are an even number of zircons and sapphires, but a greater number of sapphires. There are fewer agates than rubies. There are 3 more garnets than pearls.

Answers on page 185.

GLOBE QUEST

Fly from Miami to Seattle, visiting each city once. See if you can find the cheapest route for your trip. Less than $435 would make you a Super Vacationer; less than $420, a Passport Pioneer; less than $400, a Seasoned Traveler. If you can make the trip for $340, then you're a Globe Quester!

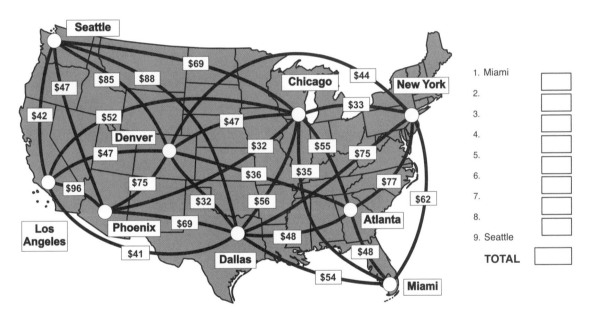

1. Miami

2.

3.

4.

5.

6.

7.

8.

9. Seattle

TOTAL

Answers on page 186.

BIRD PHOTOGRAPHY

Gufferton Springs recently hired 5 wildlife photographers to capture some local birds on film for use in an upcoming tourism brochure. Each photographer was assigned a specific type of bird to photograph, and although they all went to Gufferton Springs Nature Preserve on the same morning, each photographer arrived there at a different time. Four of the 5 photographers were successful in capturing their assigned bird on film. Using only the following clues, match each photographer to the bird they were assigned, determine how many photos they were able to take during their excursion, and figure out what time they entered the nature preserve.

1. Kevin wasn't the last to enter the nature preserve, and he didn't come back with exactly 12 photographs.

2. The photographer who failed to snap any photos arrived at the preserve sometime before the one who photographed the vultures.

3. The woodpecker photographer (who wasn't Janice) arrived sometime before the one assigned to capture some osprey on film (who didn't return with exactly 12 photographs).

4. Of Kaitlyn and the photographer who was sent to capture pictures of a scarlet tanager, one came back with just 5 photographs, and the other was the third photographer to enter the preserve.

5. The 5 photographers were: the one who was sent to photograph a titmouse, the one who returned with the most photographs, Victor, and the last 2 to arrive at the preserve.

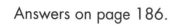

6. Of the photographer who arrived earliest at the nature preserve and the one who snapped the most photographs, one went looking for vultures and the other for scarlet tanagers.

Answers on page 186.

Time	Birdwatcher	Photographs	Bird
6:30 A.M.			
7:00 A.M.			
8:15 A.M.			
8:45 A.M.			
9:30 A.M.			

		Birdwatcher					Photographs					Bird				
		Janice	Kaitlyn	Kevin	Peter	Victor	0	3	5	12	29	Osprey	Scarlet Tanager	Titmouse	Vulture	Woodpecker
Time	6:30 A.M.															
	7:00 A.M.															
	8:15 A.M.															
	8:45 A.M.															
	9:30 A.M.															
Bird	Osprey															
	Scarlet Tanager															
	Titmouse															
	Vulture															
	Woodpecker															
Photographs	0															
	3															
	5															
	12															
	29															

Answers on page 186.

MEND THE BRIDGES

Rain has swept through the entire county, flooding all the bridges indicated by circles. Your job is to travel to each location—A through I, in any order—by restoring only 2 of the bridges.

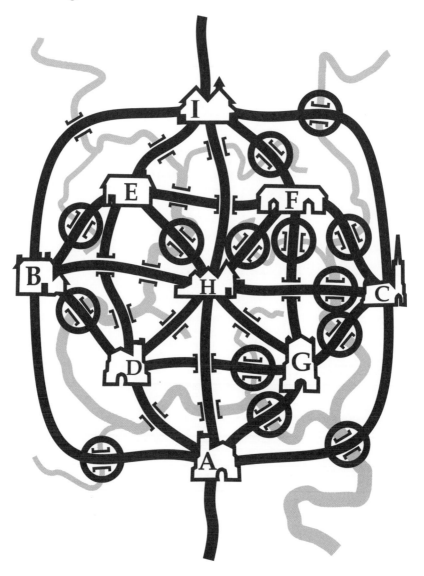

Answers on page 186.

LIAR'S LOGIC!

Use the following information to figure out who is lying and who is telling the truth. There are 3 truth tellers and 2 liars.

Person A says person C is telling the truth.

Person B says person A is lying.

Person C says person B is lying.

Person D says person B is telling the truth.

Person E says person D is telling the truth.

OVERHEARD INFORMATION (PART I)

Read the story below, than turn the page and answer the questions.

The investigator overheard the thief telling his accomplice where the stolen loot was stored—on 41 S. 6th Street, on the 4th floor, in the 2nd room on the left, in a safe with the combination 34-43-434.

Answers on page 186.

OVERHEARD INFORMATION (PART II)

(Do not read this until you have read the previous page!)

The investigator overheard the information about where the stolen loot was stored, but didn't have anywhere to write it down! Answer the questions below to help him remember.

1. What was the street address?

    A. 41 N. 6th St.

    B. 41 S. 6th St.

    C. 6 N. 41st St.

    D. 6 S. 41st St.

2. What floor?

    A. 1st

    B. 2nd

    C. 3rd

    D. 4th

3. Was the room on the left or the right side of the hallway?

    A. Left

    B. Right

4. What was the combination to the safe?

    A. 43-34-434

    B. 34-34-434

    C. 34-43-434

    D. 34-43-343

Answers on page 186.

DON'T MISS THE BUS (PART I)

There won't be a quiz at school today, but there will be one on the school bus. First, study this picture for 2 minutes. Then turn the page and answer the 10 questions. Seven or more correct answers puts you in the driver's seat.

DON'T MISS THE BUS (PART II)

(Do not read this until you have read the previous page!)

1. How many kids are standing?

2. What shape are the earrings that the bus driver is wearing?

3. The girl with the braids is sitting in what row from the front?

4. What can be seen on the front lawn of the house in the side window?

5. What are the initials on the cap of the person wearing sunglasses?

6. Where are the hands of the kid who is blowing a bubble?

7. Who can be seen through the back window of the bus?

8. What is the name of the book sticking out of the standing boy's backpack?

9. What is in the right hand of the kid holding the lunch box?

10. The kid with his feet in the air has how many shoes on?

Answers on page 187.

GLOBE QUEST

Fly from Miami to Seattle, visiting each city once. See if you can find the cheapest route for your trip. Less than $360 would make you a Super Vacationer; less than $350, a Passport Pioneer; less than $329, a Seasoned Traveler. If you can make the trip for $290, then you're a Globe Quester!

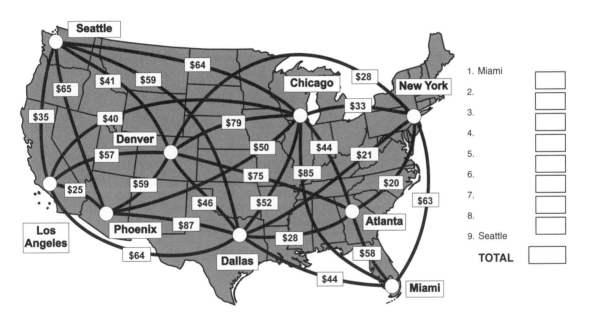

1. Miami

2. ☐

3. ☐

4. ☐

5. ☐

6. ☐

7. ☐

8. ☐

9. Seattle ☐

TOTAL ☐

Answers on page 187.

CRYPTO-LOGIC

Each of the numbers in the sequence below represents a letter. Use the mathematical clues to determine which number stands for which letter and reveal the encrypted word.

Hint: Remember that a / indicates divided by, and that all sums in parentheses must be done first.

8 1 4 4 3

Clues:

R=10   E-W=T

I=(R/2)-3   2T=L

2I=E   L+I=S

E/E=W

RACE TO THE TRUTH

Can you determine the order of the 7 runners in the race based on the information below?

Chuck placed in the top 3 runners. Tiffany was not one of the last 3 runners. There were 3 other runners between Geraldine and Lorenzo. Lorenzo was directly ahead of Mina. Albert, who came in sometime behind Geraldine, beat out at least 3 other runners, including Tiffany. There were 4 runners between Chuck and Dexter.

Answers on page 187.

SPY FLY

As an international spy, your mission is to travel from your headquarters at Seth Castle to your safe house at Faro. To disguise your trail, you must stop once—and only once—at each airport. See if you can find the cheapest route for your trip. Less than $310 would make you a Steady Sleuth; less than $300, a Cool Operator; less than $290, a Crafty Agent. If you can make it on $280, then you're a Super Spy!

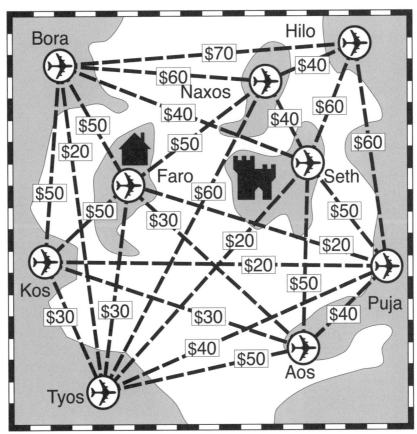

Answers on page 187.

A MUSICAL DISCOVERY

Scholars recently unearthed a folio of previously unknown sonatas written in the 19th century by a composer known only as "Z." We know that he worked on his music only for a period of 5 years between 1863 and 1867 and that he had the habit of naming his compositions after women he admired. This new folio contained 5 sonatas, each of a different type (flute, piano, violin, etc.) and each in a different key (A minor, C major, etc.). Using only the clues below, determine the type, title, and key of each sonata, as well as the year in which "Z" composed it.

1. The earliest of the 5 sonatas was in either C minor or D minor.

2. *Margot* was composed one year before the sonata in C major, which wasn't named *Eliza*.

3. Of *Heloise* and the clarinet sonata (which wasn't the earliest of the 5 pieces), one was in D minor and the other was composed in 1865.

4. The piano sonata wasn't in the key of C minor.

5. Either the flute sonata or the one composed in 1864 was in C major.

6. The 1865 sonata was titled either *Theresa* or *Heloise*.

7. The 1866 cello sonata, which was named after the infamous Lady Margot Winthorpe, wasn't in A minor.

8. Neither *Beatrice* nor the C major sonata was written in 1863.

9. *Beatrice* was composed one year after the violin sonata.

Year	Title	Instrument	Key
1863			
1864			
1865			
1866			
1867			

		Title					Instrument					Key				
		Beatrice	Eliza	Heloise	Margot	Theresa	Cello	Clarinet	Flute	Piano	Violin	A minor	C major	C minor	D minor	E minor
Year	1863															
	1864															
	1865															
	1866															
	1867															
Key	A minor															
	C major															
	C minor															
	D minor															
	E minor															
Instrument	Cello															
	Clarinet															
	Flute															
	Piano															
	Violin															

Answers on page 187.

ROOK JUMPING

Make a series of jumps from start to finish, moving like a rook chess piece (up, down, sideways, but not diagonally). The number in the corner of each cell indicates the distance of each jump. Write the sequence of your jumps in the cells (1, 2, 3, etc.). Solve with the fewest jumps.

1 **START**	4	4	1	2	4
3	2	1	5	5	1
2	4	2	4	3	2
3	4	2	2	5	3
2	2	2	4	5	3
5	4	4	3	2	0 **FINISH**

Answers on page 187.

A PASSION FOR FASHION (PART I)

Study these wearable items for a minute, then turn the page for a memory challenge.

Tank top

Platform shoes

Bell-bottoms

Cargo pants

Ball gown

Turtleneck sweater

Overalls

Pearls

A PASSION FOR FASHION (PART II)

Do not read this until you have read the previous page!

Check off the items you saw on the previous page.

___ Mao jacket

___ Camisole

___ Tank top

___ Overalls

___ Capri pants

___ Bolero jacket

___ Bell-bottoms

___ Earrings

___ Platform shoes

___ Bermuda shorts

___ Turtleneck sweater

___ Miniskirt

___ Cargo pants

___ Tube top

Answers on page 188.

GLOBE QUEST

Fly from Miami to Seattle, visiting each city on this map once. See if you can find the cheapest route for your trip. Less than $377 would make you a Super Vacationer; less than $338, a Passport Pioneer; less than $310, a Seasoned Traveler. If you can make the trip for $261, then you're a Globe Quester!

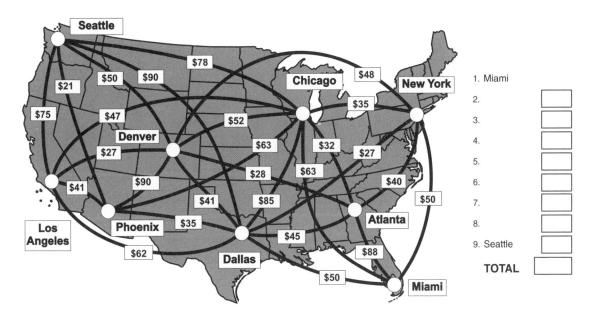

1. Miami

2. ☐

3. ☐

4. ☐

5. ☐

6. ☐

7. ☐

8. ☐

9. Seattle ☐

TOTAL ☐

Answers on page 188.

OLYMPIAN COACHES

The North Yukon Hockey Association (NYHA) held a banquet this weekend to honor a select group of team coaches, each of whom had been a member of the national hockey team during a different Winter Olympics. Each of these ex-Olympians now coaches a different NYHA league team. Using the clues below, match each coach to their current team, and determine which Winter Olympics they participated in and what year they began their NYHA coaching career.

1. Neither Adrian May nor the Timberwolves coach started their career in 2001.

2. The 1994 Winter Olympian didn't start his coaching career in 2005.

3. Between Jim Welch and the Ozlanders coach, one was in the 1998 Olympics and the other started coaching in 2001. The Kestrels coach wasn't in either the 1980 or the 1994 Olympics.

4. Dyson Pyre (who wasn't in the 1988 Olympics) started coaching one year after Jim Welch began his coaching career.

5. The coach for the Red Hawks wasn't in the 1980 Winter Olympics.

6. The coach who was on the 1984 Olympic team (who wasn't Calvin Bash) started coaching sometime before Jim Welch.

7. The Timberwolves coach began coaching one year after the Ozlanders coach began his career.

8. Between Adrian May and the Olympian who started coaching in 2002, one was in the 1994 Olympics and the other was in the 1998 Olympics.

Year Joined	Coach	Olympics	Hockey Team
2001			
2002			
2003			
2004			
2005			

		Coach					Olympics					Hockey Team				
		Calvin Bash	Fred Heche	Adrian May	Dyson Pyre	Jim Welch	1980	1984	1988	1994	1998	Black Wings	Kestrels	Ozlanders	Red Hawks	Timberwolves
Year Joined	2001															
	2002															
	2003															
	2004															
	2005															
Hockey Team	Black Wings															
	Kestrels															
	Ozlanders															
	Red Hawks															
	Timberwolves															
Olympics	1980															
	1984															
	1988															
	1994															
	1998															

Answers on page 188.

EQUIPMENT MIXUP

George Griffin, the hockey team's equipment manager, is in a bit of a pickle. It was his job to order 5 pairs of ice skates for 5 of the team's star players, and although he has a list of 5 shoe sizes, 5 brand names, and 5 shoelace colors requested by each player, he neglected to write down which player requested each size, brand, and color! Help him match each player to the shoe size, brand name, and shoelace color they requested, using the clues provided below.

1. Jonathan didn't request Trembley skates.

2. The silver laces are intended for either the size 9.5 or size 10 skates.

3. Between Jonathan and the player who requested Chesterton skates, one wanted black laces and the other has the smallest shoe size of all 5 players.

4. Michael's skates are one-half size larger than the player who asked for white laces.

5. Nathaniel didn't want Slimline skates and didn't request black laces.

6. Bennett doesn't wear size 10 skates.

7. Between Michael and the player with the second-largest shoe size, one requested Ice-Pro skates and the other wanted blue laces.

8. The player who wanted the blue laces has smaller feet than the one who wanted Slimline skates.

9. Jonathan's skates are one-half size smaller than Michael's.

10. The player who asked for black laces is one-half size larger than the one who requested silver laces.

Shoe Size	Player	Brand Name	Lace Color
9			
9.5			
10			
10.5			
11			

		Player					Brand Name					Lace Color				
		Bennett	Bryan	Jonathan	Michael	Nathaniel	Chesterton	Hockeymate	Ice-Pro	Slimline	Trembley	black	gold	blue	silver	white
Shoe Size	9															
	9.5															
	10															
	10.5															
	11															
Lace Color	black															
	gold															
	blue															
	silver															
	white															
Brand Name	Chesterton															
	Hockeymate															
	Ice-Pro															
	Slimline															
	Trembley															

Answers on page 188.

SINS & VIRTUES

The local Bible study group decided to do something a little different for next week. Each member of the Bible study was given one of the deadly sins and cardinal virtues to learn about, but no one was given corresponding sins and virtues. The next week, each member would present what they learned to the rest of the group. Determine the full name of each group member, and the deadly sin and cardinal virtue that each was assigned.

1. Ms. Carlson wasn't given greed. Harold was given envy but not temperance.

2. Beth's last name isn't Lorenson and she didn't learn about humility. Pride and patience were given to Mr. West and Allison, in no particular order.

3. Ms. Holding, whose first name isn't Sofia, learned about temperance but not about wrath or gluttony. One woman was given chastity and gluttony.

4. The man who got sloth also got kindness. Mr. Brooks, whose first name isn't Andrew, didn't learn about wrath.

5. Elliot's last name isn't West. Allison was given greed but the corresponding virtue was given to Mr. Brooks.

6. The seven deadly sins were given to Marcia, Mr. Severn, the one who learned about gluttony, the one who learned about diligence, Ms. Parker, Harold, and the one who learned about wrath.

First Name	Last Name	Deadly Sin	Cardinal Virtue

		First Name							Cardinal Virtue							Deadly Sin						
		Allison	Andrew	Beth	Elliot	Harold	Marcia	Sofia	Charity	Chastity	Diligence	Humility	Kindness	Patience	Temperance	Envy	Gluttony	Greed	Lust	Pride	Sloth	Wrath
Last Name	Brooks																					
	Carlson																					
	Holding																					
	Lorenson																					
	Parker																					
	Severn																					
	West																					
Deadly Sin	Envy												X									
	Gluttony														X							
	Greed								X													
	Lust									X												
	Pride											X										
	Sloth										X											
	Wrath													X								
Cardinal Virtue	Charity																					
	Chastity																					
	Diligence																					
	Humility																					
	Kindness																					
	Patience																					
	Temperance																					

Answers on page 188.

UP IN SMOKE

There's a thief in this man's midst—and he's stolen his best cigars! See if you can focus your visual acuity and spot the cigar thief.

Answers on page 188.

ROBBER RIDDLE

Cryptograms are messages in substitution code. Break the code to read the riddle and its answer. For example, THE SMART CAT might become FVO QWGDF JGF if F is substituted for T, V for H, O for E, and so on.

SDU SWO PDA PDEAB WHH SAP?

DA PNEAZ PK NKX A NERANXWJG.

BOOKSTORE BROWSE

Can you determine the order of the bookstore sections based on the information below?

You are walking through a bookstore and pass through 7 distinct sections. The science fiction section is one of the first 3 sections you pass. Travel is one of the last 3 sections, but not the last. You pass through the classics section immediately after browsing through biography. Romance is right next to travel, either immediately before or immediately after. After you pass through classics, you walk through three other sections before reaching the young adult fiction. The cookbooks section follows the young adult section.

Answers on page 188.

SPY FLY

As an international spy, your mission is to travel from your headquarters at Seth Castle to your safe house at Faro. To disguise your trail, you must stop once—and only once—at each airport. See if you can find the cheapest route for your trip. Less than $300 would make you a Steady Sleuth; less than $290, a Cool Operator; less than $280, a Crafty Agent. If you can make it on $270, then you're a Super Spy!

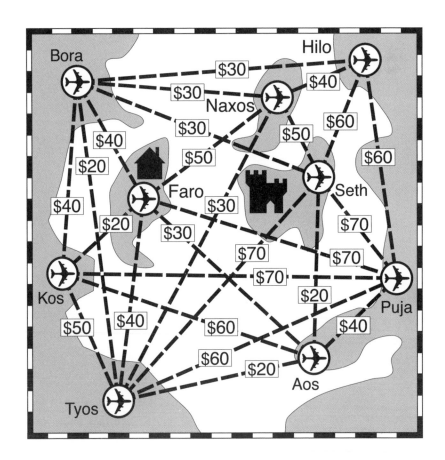

= Airport
= Start
= Finish

Answers on page 189.

CRYPTO-LOGIC

Each of the numbers in the sequence below represents a letter. Use the mathematical clues to determine which number stands for which letter and reveal the encrypted word.

Hint: Remember that a / indicates divided by, and that all sums in parentheses must be done first.

$$8\ 4\ 9\ 3\ 2\ 1\ 7$$

Clues:
O squared = O + O	2R = T
½O = V	2P / 3 = T
P + V = 10	R + (R / 3) = M
P – O = E	2M = I

NUMBER NOGGIN-SCRATCHER (PART I)

Look at the list of numerals below for 1 minute, and then turn the page.

$$634563312377896$$

Answers on page 189.

NUMBER NOGGIN-SCRATCHER (PART II)

(Do not read this until you have read the previous page!)

What was the longest string of consecutive numbers in the string of numbers on the previous page?

A. 123   D. 3456

B. 1234   E. 6789

C. 345   F. 789

GEMSTONE MATH

There are 8 types of gems. There is 1 gem of the first type, 2 of the second type, 3 of the third type, 4 of the fourth type, 5 of the fifth type, 6 of the sixth type, 7 of the seventh type, and 8 of the eighth type. From the information given below, can you tell how many gemstones there are of each kind?

There are even numbers of amethysts and opals. There are odd numbers of diamonds and pearls. There is 1 more emerald than there are pieces of jade. There are exactly half as many opals as there are emeralds. There is 1 more garnet than there are pearls. There are 2 fewer pieces of turquoise than there are diamonds. There are fewer than 8 garnets. There is more than 1 pearl.

Answers on page 189.

GLOBE QUEST

Fly from Miami to Seattle, visiting each city once. See if you can find the cheapest route for your trip. Less than $440 would make you a Super Vacationer; less than $400, a Passport Pioneer; less than $380, a Seasoned Traveler. If you can make the trip for $350, then you're a Globe Quester!

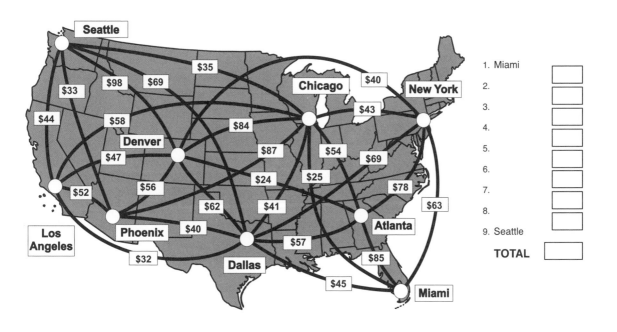

1. Miami

2. ☐

3. ☐

4. ☐

5. ☐

6. ☐

7. ☐

8. ☐

9. Seattle

TOTAL ☐

Answers on page 189.

HOCKEY SCHEDULE

Danny and Denise invited several friends over to watch an entire day of hockey on their brand-new 60" HD television. They couldn't have picked a better day—there are 5 different games airing at different times and on different channels. Using the clues below, figure out which teams play at which starting times, and which cable channels air each of those games.

1. The Dolphins game has the latest start time.

2. The THN game (which doesn't feature the Ewings) begins 90 minutes after the game that starts on ESPT II.

3. The Sharks game doesn't air on ESPT I.

4. The Quests game begins 90 minutes after the Patriots game starts.

5. Between the Brahmins game and the one that airs on THN, one begins at 2:30 P.M. and the other features the Timberwolves.

6. The Bees game begins 90 minutes after the HLH game.

7. Between the Sharks game and the one that begins at 1:00 P.M., one features the Dolphins and the other airs on THN.

Game Time	Home Team	Away Team	Channel
11:30 A.M.			
1:00 P.M.			
2:30 P.M.			
4:00 P.M.			
5:30 P.M.			

		Home Team					Away Team					Channel				
		Bees	Brahmins	Coyotes	Dolphins	Ewings	Patriots	Quests	Ravens	Sharks	Timberwolves	ESPT I	ESPT II	HLH	STN	THN
Game Time	11:30 A.M.															
	1:00 P.M.															
	2:30 P.M.															
	4:00 P.M.															
	5:30 P.M.															
Channel	ESPT I															
	ESPT II															
	HLH															
	STN															
	THN															
Away Team	Patriots															
	Quests															
	Ravens															
	Sharks															
	Timberwolves															

Answers on page 189.

SPY FLY

As an international spy, your mission is to travel from your headquarters at Seth Castle to your safe house at Faro. To disguise your trail, you must stop once—and only once—at each airport. See if you can find the cheapest route for your trip. Less than $220 would make you a Steady Sleuth; less than $190, a Cool Operator; less than $160, a Crafty Agent. If you can make it on $130, then you're a Super Spy!

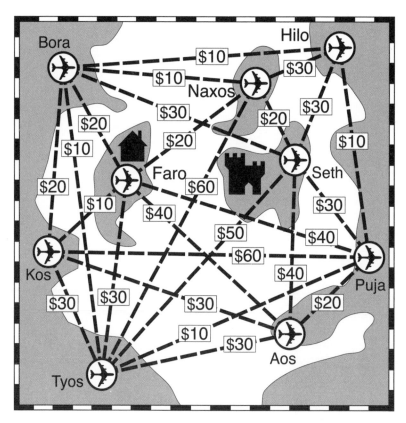

ROOK JUMPING

Make a series of jumps from start to finish, moving like a rook chess piece (up, down, sideways, but not diagonally). The number in the corner of each cell indicates the distance of each jump. Write the sequence of your jumps in the cells (1, 2, 3, etc.). Solve with the fewest jumps.

21 jumps: Cautious Castle

20 jumps: Cunning Castle

19 jumps: Crafty Castle

18 jumps: Master Rook

1 START	4	4	1	2	4
3	2	1	5	5	1
2	4	2	4	3	2
3	4	2	2	5	3
2	2	5	4	5	3
5	4	4	3	2	0 FINISH

Answers on page 190.

JAPANESE TEA SHOP

Five friends each met at *Zen-mai-cha*, an upscale tea shop that offers several different kinds of imported Japanese tea. Each tea sold at the shop is priced by the ounce, and every tea has a different price. After sampling several different varieties, each of the 5 friends purchased a different amount of the tea they liked most. Using only the clues below, determine the price and type of tea each person bought, as well as how many ounces each purchased.

1. The most expensive of the 5 teas was either the genmaicha or the bancha.

2. Uriel's tea cost more than the bancha.

3. Of Xander and the one who paid $3.75 for their tea, one chose the kukicha and the other purchased the smallest amount of tea of all 5 friends.

4. Neither the tea that cost $3.75/oz nor the one that was purchased in a full 16-ounce tin was the hojicha.

5. The tea that was purchased in the 12-ounce tin cost 50 cents less per ounce than the gyokuro.

6. The person who bought 16 ounces of tea (who wasn't Richard) didn't select the genmaicha.

7. The tea that was purchased in the 10-ounce tin cost 50 cents less per ounce than the one Uriel bought (at the highest price).

8. The hojicha was purchased in 5 ounces.

9. The 5 teas were the ones that cost $3.25/oz and $4.25/oz, the genmaicha, the one Matthew chose, and the one purchased by the friend who bought only five ounces of tea (which didn't cost $3.75/oz).

Prices	Customers	Teas	Amounts
$2.75/oz			
$3.25/oz			
$3.75/oz			
$4.25/oz			
$4.75/oz			

		Customers					Teas					Amounts				
		Brian	Matthew	Richard	Uriel	Xander	Bancha	Genmaicha	Gyokuro	Hojicha	Kukicha	5 ounces	7 ounces	10 ounces	12 ounces	16 ounces
Prices	$2.75/oz															
	$3.25/oz															
	$3.75/oz															
	$4.25/oz															
	$4.75/oz															
Amounts	5 ounces															
	7 ounces															
	10 ounces															
	12 ounces															
	16 ounces															
Teas	Bancha															
	Genmaicha															
	Gyokuro															
	Hojicha															
	Kukicha															

Answers on page 190.

MEND THE BRIDGES

Rain has swept through the entire county, flooding all the bridges indicated by circles. Your job is to travel to each location—A through I, in any order—by restoring only 2 of the bridges.

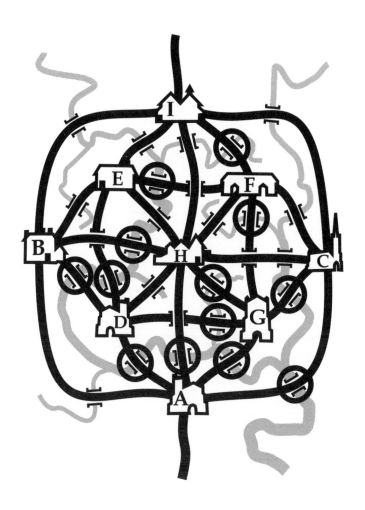

Answers on page 190.

LIAR'S LOGIC!

Decipher the statements below using the following information to figure out who is lying and who is telling the truth. There are 3 truth tellers and 2 liars.

Person A says, "Person B is called Bernie and I'm Alf."

Person B says, "Person C is called Colin and I'm Bernie."

Person C says, "Person D is called Donald and I'm Carl."

Person D says, "Person E is called Eli and I'm Dan."

Person E says, "Person C is called Carl and I'm Ed."

Whose name can we be sure of, if any?

Answers on page 190.

GLOBE QUEST

Fly from Miami to Seattle, visiting each city once. See if you can find the cheapest route for your trip. Less than $360 would make you a Super Vacationer; less than $340, a Passport Pioneer; less than $309, a Seasoned Traveler. If you can make the trip for $255, then you're a Globe Quester!

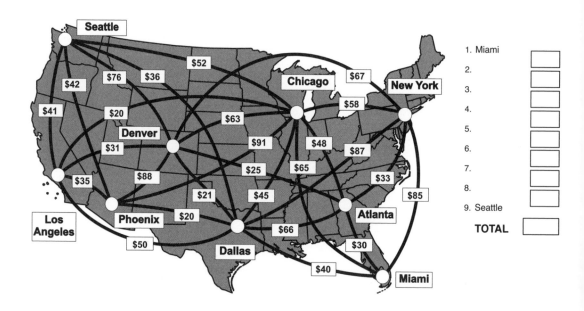

Globe Quest9013_p.eps

1. Miami
2.
3.
4.
5.
6.
7.
8.
9. Seattle

TOTAL

Answers on page 190.

SPY FLY

As an international spy, your mission is to travel from your headquarters at Seth Castle to your safe house at Faro. To disguise your trail, you must stop once—and only once—at each airport. See if you can find the cheapest route for your trip. Less than $290 would make you a Steady Sleuth; less than $280, a Cool Operator; less than $270, a Crafty Agent. If you can make it on $260, then you're a Super Spy!

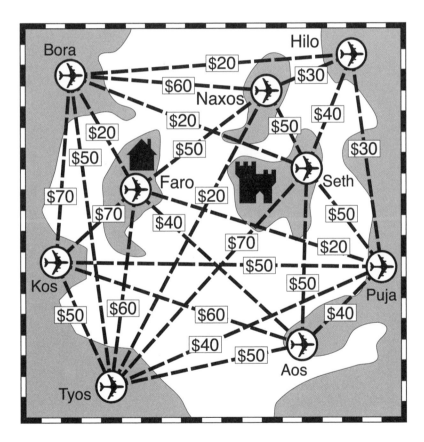

= Airport
= Start
= Finish

Answers on page 190.

A DAY AT THE RACES

The centerpiece of the Westchester County Fair—the big pig race—was a rousing success this year. Five pigs were entered in the contest, with each assigned its own number. Using the clues below, determine the order in which the 5 prize-winning pigs finished the race, the owner of each pig, and the racing number assigned to each:

1. Of Terrence's pig and the pig with the highest racing number (which wasn't Squiggles), one finished second (but didn't wear #3) and the other was named Pinky.

2. Squiggles didn't finish first.

3. Emily's pig didn't wear #8.

4. Of Emily's pig and the pig that finished in fifth place (which wore #6), one was named Rutager and the other Squiggles.

5. Makenna's pig wore #6.

6. The pig wearing #8 finished sometime after the pig wearing #9.

7. Of Paul's pig and the fourth-place finisher, one wore #11 and the other was named Charlotte.

8. Neither Emily's pig nor the pig named Rutager wore #3.

9. Hamlet came in second.

Places	Owners	Pigs	Numbers
First			
Second			
Third			
Fourth			
Fifth			

		Owners					Pigs					Numbers				
		Emily	Kendra	Makenna	Paul	Terrence	Charlotte	Hamlet	Pinky	Rutager	Squiggles	#3	#6	#8	#9	#11
Places	First															
	Second															
	Third															
	Fourth															
	Fifth															
Numbers	#3											
	#6											
	#8											
	#9											
	#11											
Pigs	Charlotte						
	Hamlet						
	Pinky						
	Rutager						
	Squiggles						

Answers on page 191.

ROBBER RIDDLE

Cryptograms are messages in substitution code. Break the code to read the riddle and its answer. For example, THE SMART CAT might become FVO QWGDF JGF if F is substituted for T, V for H, O for E, and so on.

OZQ VAV LZW LZAWX GFDQ KSQ "EWGO"

LG LZW HGDAUW?

TWUSMKW ZW OSK S USL TMJYDSJ.

RESTAURANT RIDDLE

Can you determine the order of the restaurants on the street based on the information below?

There are seven restaurants on the street that you're walking down. The Korean barbeque is neither the first place you pass nor at the end of the street. The pizza place, the ice cream parlor, and the sandwich place are all in a row, in that order. There is one other restaurant between the sushi place and the Mexican restaurant. After the burger joint, you pass two restaurants before you reach the pizza place. The sushi restaurant is one of the first three restaurants.

Answers on page 191.

GEMSTONE MATH

There are 8 types of gems. There is 1 gem of the first type, 2 of the second type, 3 of the third type, 4 of the fourth type, 5 of the fifth type, 6 of the sixth type, 7 of the seventh type, and 8 of the eighth type. From the information given below, can you tell how many gemstones there are of each kind?

There are twice as many garnets as rubies. There are more amethysts than rubies. There are 4 more sapphires than emeralds. There are at least 6 opals. There are fewer diamonds than rubies. There is 1 more pearl than there are garnets. There are twice as many opals as garnets.

ANTE UP

What is the largest amount listed below that could NOT be wagered (in exact, whole dollar amounts) if you had only $5 and $6 chips?

    A. $8.00

    B. $19.00

    C. $47.00

    D. $119.00

Answers on page 191.

TREASURE HUNT

The treasure hunter visited nine cities, finding a clue in each one that led her to the treasure in the final city. Can you put the list of the nine cities she visited in order, using the information below?

There were exactly three other cities visited between Paris and Jakarta.

There was at least one city visited between London and Pretoria.

Paris was not the first city visited, and Jakarta was not the last.

Singapore was visited sometime after London and sometime before Cairo and Sydney.

Cairo was visited after London, but not immediately afterward.

The city in Indonesia was visited immediately before the city in Australia, which was visited before either South American city.

There were four cities visited between Pretoria and Buenos Aires.

The treasure was found in Rio de Janeiro.

Answers on page 191.

NOT SO HAPPY BIRTHDAY

Molly had heard that "40 is the new 30," but she didn't believe it and wanted to stay in her 30s for a while longer. As usual, when her husband Homer tried to understand it, he instead stuck his foot in his mouth and said something that made it worse. After doing the math on a piece of paper, Homer said to Molly: "The day before yesterday, you were 39 years old. But next year, you will be 42." Molly realized he was right but hit him with a pillow anyway. How did Molly not only leave her 30s, but skip a couple of years in the process, too?

NUMBER NOGGIN-SCRATCHER (PART I)

Look at the list of numerals below for 1 minute, and then turn the page.

672333434987012212

Answers on page 191.

NUMBER NOGGIN-SCRATCHER (PART II)

(Do not read this until you have read the previous page!)

Which one of the following groups of 3 numbers began the sequence on the previous page?

A. 723 B. 673 C. 672 D. 434 E. 212

SHE'S A RICH GIRL

In a new twist on blind dates, a single woman who had just won $100,000 in the lottery offered to date to the first man who could guess her name. Since the woman wanted to date a smart guy, not just one who could say names really fast, she gave the following hint: Assign the letters of the alphabet to their numerical values. That means A = 1, B = 2, C = 3, up to Z = 26. Her first name has the letter values that, when multiplied together, equal exactly 100,000. While Louie the lounge lizard tried all of the names of women who had ever turned him down, Mike the macho mathematician got her name, the date, her heart, and a pre-nup. What was the woman's name?

Answers on page 191.

ROUND AND ROUND WE GO (PART I)

Look at the pictures and remember the names of the objects.

ROUND AND ROUND WE GO (PART II)

(Do not read this until you have read the previous page!)

Put a check by the words you saw on the preceding page:

FRYING PAN

SMILEY FACE

EARTH

COOKIE

MARBLE

PIZZA

HELM

PANCAKE

BASEBALL

BASKETBALL

GOLF BALL

SOCCER BALL

STOPWATCH

Answers on page 191.

GLOBE QUEST

Fly from Miami to Seattle, visiting each city once. See if you can find the cheapest route for your trip. Less than $425 would make you a Super Vacationer; less than $415, a Passport Pioneer; less than $380, a Seasoned Traveler. If you can make the trip for $318, then you're a Globe Quester!

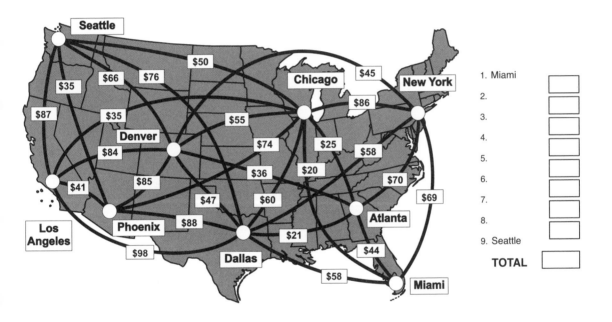

1. Miami

2.

3.

4.

5.

6.

7.

8.

9. Seattle

TOTAL

Answers on page 192.

CRYPTO-LOGIC

Each of the numbers in the sequence below represents a letter. Use the mathematical clues to determine which number stands for which letter and reveal the encrypted word.

Hint: Remember that a / indicates divided by, and that all sums in parentheses must be done first.

$$7\ 3\ 5\ 3\ 9\ 6\ 2\ 8\ 3$$

Clues: The value equal to the number of times it is present represents E

T squared is 12E   S x P = P

I squared + I = T   D + C = P + E

P - S = V   D > T

V = 2 x I squared

GEMSTONE MATH

There are 7 types of gems. There is 1 gem of the first type, 2 of the second type, 3 of the third type, 4 of the fourth type, 5 of the fifth type, 6 of the sixth type, and 7 of the seventh type. From the information given below, can you tell how many gemstones there are of each kind?

There are 4 more pearls than opals. There are 4 more peridots than diamonds. There are twice as many amethysts as diamonds. There are even numbers of emeralds and aquamarines. There is an odd number of pearls. There are fewer aquamarines than amethysts or emeralds. There are fewer opals than diamonds.

Answers on page 192.

MEND THE BRIDGES

...ain has swept through the entire county, flooding all the bridges indicated by ...ircles. Your job is to travel to each location—A through I, in any order—by restor-...g only 2 of the bridges.

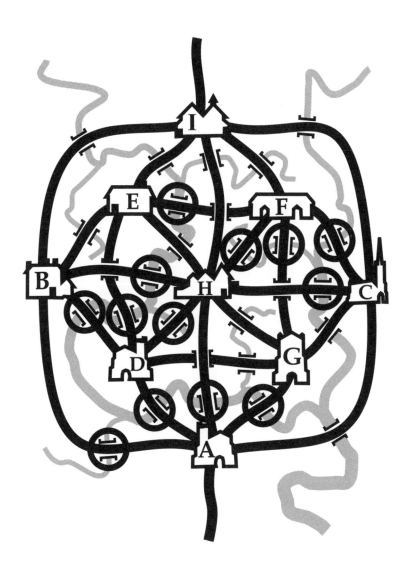

Answers on page 192.

SCIENCE STROLL

Can you determine the order of the booths at the school science fair based on the information below?

You are walking past a line of 8 booths at the science fair. You pass 3 exhibits after the miniature volcano before you reach the robot exhibit. You pass the ant farm before you pass the solar system model, which you pass before you reach the plant seedlings. The fossil exhibit is one of the 2 final exhibits. You pass 4 exhibits after the solar system model before you reach the circuit board display. You pass the miniature bridge and the next booth that displays the plant seedlings before you reach the fossil exhibit, but there is one booth between the plant seedlings and the fossils. You pass 2 exhibits after the ant farm before you reach the miniature bridge.

SPENDING ACCOUNT

Mitzi has $513 to spend. She spends ⁴⁄₉ of the $513 in the morning on clothes, 60 percent of the remainder in the afternoon on jewelry, and writes out a check for $74 for dining out. What is her financial situation at the end of the day?

Answers on page 192.

GOOD-LOOKING LOGIC

Five good-looking guys went shopping at the Gadgets for Good-Looking Guys electronics store. Each good-looking guy walked out of Gadgets for Good-Looking Guys with a different electronic gadget for his good-looking home. Each good-looking guy went to his good-looking home and installed his electronic gadget in a different room of the house than the other good-looking guys did. Here's some of the things the good-looking guys did:

Mr. Clooney did not install his gadget in his bedroom.

Mr. Depp bought a PC.

Tom installed his gadget in his bathroom.

Mr. Cruise bought a robot vacuum.

Johnny bought a global positioning system.

Tom did not install his gadget in his bedroom.

George did not buy a DVD player.

Matt installed his gadget in his kitchen.

Johnny did not install his gadget in his living room.

Mr. Pitt installed his gadget in his attic.

Mr. Damon did not install his gadget in his kitchen.

Brad bought a wide-screen TV.

What was each good-looking guy's first and last name, what electronic gadget did each buy, and in what room of their good-looking house did each install his gadget?

Answers on page 192.

SPY FLY

As an international spy, your mission is to travel from your headquarters at Seth Castle to your safe house at Faro. To disguise your trail, you must stop once—and only once—at each airport. See if you can find the cheapest route for your trip. Less than $270 would make you a Steady Sleuth; less than $260, a Cool Operator; less than $240, a Crafty Agent. If you can make it on $230, then you're a Super Spy!

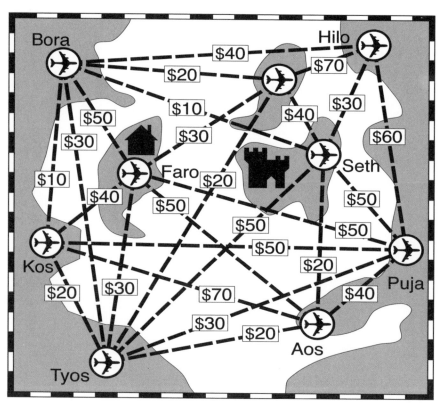

= Airport
= Start
= Finish

Answers on page 192.

ANSWER KEY

Motel Hideout (page 4)

The thief is in room 25.

Prime Suspect (page 5)

	Nationality	Hair	Coat	Build
1	Italian	none	green	round
2	English	red	blue	thin
3	Chinese	gray	purple	slim
4	Spanish	white	cream	medium
5	African	dark	yellow	hunched
6	Mexican	brown	mauve	fat

Liar's Logic! (page 6)

The liars are A, B, and D. If E were lying, C would be a liar and B would be a truth teller, and also A would be a truth teller. But then D would also be telling the truth, making too many truth tellers. This process of elimination leaves the only possible answer as C and E as the truthful ones.

Mystery in England (page 6)

Stack the encyclopedias so you can climb on top of them and reach the key.

Password Maker (Part 1) (page 7)

See answer for Part 2.

Password Maker (Part 11) (page 8)

COWBOY GOLDEN, FREEDOM ELEPHANT, QUOTATION ORANGE, FLUTTER CAMPUS, MOUNTAIN CYMBAL, ADVICE KETTLE, PIANO LOBSTER, PRESTIGE NINETEEN, BELIEF HAMMER, CONCEPT SALAMANDER

Naughty Students (page 9)

	Name	Surname	Crime	Punishment
1	Andy	Finkel	stealing books	forfeiting sport
2	Colin	Harrow	eating in class	cleaning windows
3	Denzil	Goof	talking back	mopping floors
4	Bernard	Everong	breaking chairs	extra assignments

The Scrambled Detective (page 10)

Solve; evidence; fingerprints; footprints; fibers

Addagram (page 10)

The missing letter is I.
Forensic, thief, examine, investigate

Gemstone Math (page 11)

The count is: 1 piece of agate, 2 aquamarines, 3 peridots, 4 opals, and 5 emeralds.

Detective's Toolkit (page 11)

The order is: notepad, magnifying glass, pencil, fingerprint kit, flashlight, measuring tape

Delivery Dilemma (page 12)

	Recipient	Title 1	Title 2
1	Horsefield	Daily	Clarion
2	Graham	New	Mail
3	Fallon	Morning	Tablet
4	Jameson	Weekly	Platform
5	Illingworth	Early	Express

Relations Problem (page 13)

The relationship must be among these three possibilities.

(1) Daughter-in-law.

(2) Wife's aunt (wife's mother's brother's wife).

(3) Nephew's wife (wife's sister's son's wife).

Visual Sequence (page 13)

E. Each clock shows the time 8 hours and 7 minutes ahead of the previous one.

Spy Fly (page 14)

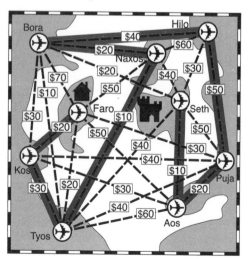

Riddle (page 15)

It got in with the greatest of ease. It was an open topped car.

Famous Detective Scramble (page 15)

1. Sherlock Holmes, E. Arthur Conan Doyle;
2. Miss Marple, C., Agatha Christie; 3. C. Auguste Dupin, D. Edgar Allan Poe; 4. Nero Wolfe, A. Rex Stout; 5. Kinsey Millhone, B. Sue Grafton

Mend the Bridges (page 16)

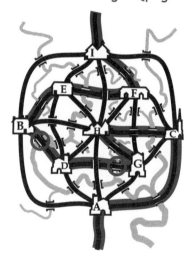

How's Your Recall? (Part I) (page 17)

See answer for Part 2.

How's Your Recall? (Part II) (page 18)

Key chain, picture frame, camp tent, opera glasses, treasure chest

Robber Riddle (page 19)

Why did the robber take a bath before going to the bank?
Because he wanted to make sure he had a clean getaway.

Race to the Truth (page 19)

The order is: Addison, Misha, Cassidy, Sloane, Blaise, Val, Dayton

Mrs. Smith's Daughters (pages 20-21)

The youngest child is not Sarah (Clue 1), Jane, or Anna (Clue 2), so it is Kate.

The oldest child is not Jane or Anna (Clue 2), so it is Sarah. Two girls are older than Anna (Clue 4), so she is 2 and Jane is 3.

Jane is the blond (Clue 4), so her eyes are brown and Anna's hair is brown (Clue 2).

Sarah does not have black hair (Clue 1), so Kate does, and Sarah is the redhead whose eyes are green (Clue 4).

Kate does not have hazel eyes (Clue 3), so her eyes are blue and 2-year-old, brown-haired Anna has hazel eyes. In summary:

Age	Name	Hair	Eyes
4	Sarah	red	green
3	Jane	blond	brown
2	Anna	brown	hazel
1	Kate	black	blue

Off Color (page 22)

	Location	Color	Painter
1	bathroom	black	Keith
2	stairway	red	Sid
3	hall	yellow	Jenny
4	kitchen	purple	Lorna

Restaurant Riddle (page 23)

On one side of the street are the Polish restaurant, the Irish pub, the Greek restaurant, and the deli. On the other side of the street are the seafood place (across from the Polish restaurant), the Thai place, the French bistro, and the Italian place.

Logical Hats (page 23)

The numbers on A and C are 10 and 5. B sees these and realizes he either has 15 or 5 on his hat. He then realizes that if he had 5 on his hat, A would have seen 5 and 5 and would have known his own hat had a 10. Since A didn't know his number, B eliminates this possibility.

Treasure Hunt (page 24)

The order is: Copenhagen (Denmark); Caracas (Venezuela); Canberra (Australia); Dakar (Senegal); Budapest (Hungary); Vientiane (Laos); Kingston (Jamaica); Nairobi (Kenya)

Lottery Tickets (page 25)

40. Each person put in $4. When 2 dropped out, there was only $32 in the pot, so each chipped in another $1 to add $8 and bring the total to $40.

Sequencing (page 25)

Surmise. The middle letter of each word represents a successive Roman numeral: I, V, X, L, C, D, M.

Liar's Logic! (page 26)

The liars are C and D. If C were telling the truth, A would be a liar, and B a liar, D would hence be a truth teller. But this would mean E had to be a liar, as he says that A tells the truth, which would be too many liars. Again, elimination leads to the only correct answer, that those telling the truth are A, B and E.

Crypto-Logic (page 26)

RIGHT

Cool Café (page 27)

	Surname	Drink	Sugars
1	Dribble	latte	1
2	Aviary	coffee	2
3	Crumple	mocha	0
4	Bloggs	tea	3

Sock Drawer (page 28)

Tom would have to pull out 3 socks. Because there are only 2 different colors, if he pulls out 3, at least 2 will be the same color.

Equalizing Heads (page 28)

Separate the coins into group A with 8 coins and group B with 15 coins. If there are x heads in group A, then there will be 15–x heads in group B. Turn over all coins in group B, and then each group will have x coins facing heads up.

It's a Shore Thing (Part I) (page 29)

See answer for Part 2.

It's a Shore Thing (Part II) (page 30)

1. flying disc; 2. conch shell; 3. Goop; 4. stripes; 5. crocodile; 6. Breeze; 7. lobster; 8. shorts, jacket, hat; 9. megaphone; 10. four

Mend the Bridges (page 31)

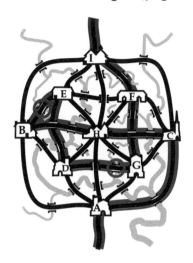

Spy Fly (page 34)

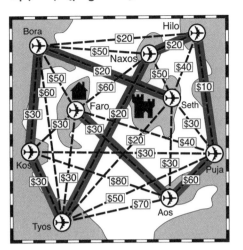

Race to the Truth (page 35)

The order is: Casey, Leticia, Tim, Chris, Eric, Amisha, Alex

Wild West (page 32)

	Name	Surname	Location	Firearm
1	Abel	Garrett	Fort Griffin	Cavalry
2	Drew	Indiana	San Antonio	Peacemaker
3	Earp	James	Red River	Schofield
4	Fingers	Hitchcock	Dodge City	Winchester
5	Butch	Lightning	Colby	Golden Boy
6	Cat	Kid	Ogallala	Derringer

The Answer's On the Money (page 35)

$1,955, because 5×17×23=1,955.

Gemstone Math (page 33)

The count is: 1 emerald, 2 pearls, 3 sapphires, 4 garnets, 5 rubies.

Treasure Hunt (page 36)

The order is: Luxembourg (Luxembourg); Moscow (Russia); Oslo (Norway); Tashkent (Uzbekistan); Washington, D.C. (United States); New Delhi (India); Montevideo (Uruguay); Ankara (Turkey)

Sequencing (page 33)

A. Ulan Bator. The pattern is that the first vowel in the gem's name is the first letter in the city's name.

A Can-Do Candle Attitude (page 37)

Dan bought 94 candles for 50 cents each, one candle for $5.50, and 5 candles for $9.50.

Overheard Information (Part I) (page 37)

See part II.

Overheard Information (Part II) (page 38)

1. The second floor; 2. The rubies; 3. underneath the carpet in the den on the third floor; 4. The opals

Library Returns (page 39)

Elliot, adventure, 4:15pm
Joel, mystery, 3:30pm
Mike, science fiction, 4:00pm
Steve, humor, 3:45pm

In the description below, each number in parenthesis refers to the clue number that the preceding statement is derived from:

The adventure book was returned at 4:15pm (3). The science fiction book was returned by Mike (5). Since the humor book was returned 15 minutes before Mike's book (2), which was returned 15 minutes before Elliot's book (4), and since Joel didn't return the adventure book (3), by elimination Elliot must have returned his book at 4:15pm. So Mike returned his book at 4:00pm and the humor book was returned at 3:45pm. Since Steve's book and the mystery book were both returned before 4:00pm, by elimination the mystery book must have been returned at 3:30pm and Steve's book at 3:45pm. Also by elimination, Joel returned his book at 3:30pm.

Library Returns (page 39) Continued

Name	Type of Book	Time Returned
Joel	Mystery	3:30 P.M.
Steve	Humor	3:45 P.M.
Mike	Science Fiction	4:00 P.M.
Elliot	Adventure	4:15 P.M.

Crypto-Logic (page 40)

TORTUROUS
F=1
N=16
O=9
R=3
S=7
T=5
U=4
P=2

Addagram (page 40)

The missing letter is I.
Diamonds, tiara, diadem, figurine

Things That Smell Good (Part I) (page 41)

See part II

Things That Smell Good (Part II) (page 42)

GARLIC, JASMINE, ONIONS, CHOW MEIN, LICORICE, CARAMEL CORN, DOUGHNUTS, CHOCOLATE

Detective Work! (page 43)

The stolen items are the hook, the fish bone, and the bear head. These items are circled on the easel.

Treasure Hunt (page 44)

The order is: Bangkok (Thailand); Dodoma (Tanzania); Madrid (Spain); Amsterdam (Netherlands); Algiers (Algeria); Lima (Peru); Skopje (Macedonia), and Tokyo (Japan).

Nice Pets (page 45)

	Owner	Pet	Name
1	Arthur	pig	Norma
2	Cathy	cat	Len
3	Evelyn	crocodile	Keith
4	Bob	rhino	Olive
5	Dennis	leopard	Molly

RBI Players (pages 46-47)

Dan had an RBI of 44. Sam Waverly didn't have an RBI of 40 and since his RBI wasn't in the 30s, by elimination Sam's RBI was 42. Therefore, Mr. Short's RBI must be 40, Jack's must be 38, and Mr. Templeton's must be 36. Also, Clark's last name is Templeton and Jack's last name is Emerald. Therefore, by elimination Mr. Short must be Mike and Dan's last name must be Case.

Spy Fly (page 48)

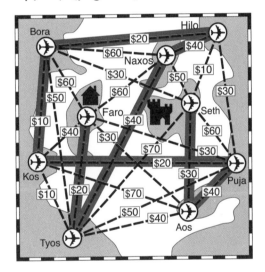

Shoe Throwing (page 49)

	Name	House Name	Road
1	Carnegie	Happy Heights	Rut Road
2	Bodman	Claptrap	Potty Place
3	Flop	Nirvana	Olive Crescent
4	Evertall	Bedlam	Nuts Close
5	Arbuthnot	Whywurry	Menice Ave
6	Dozy	Dreary	Quebec Street

Crypto-Logic (page 50)
NAME

Addagram (page 50)
The missing letter is A.
Departure, Paris, Wednesday, airplane

Spy Fly (page 51)

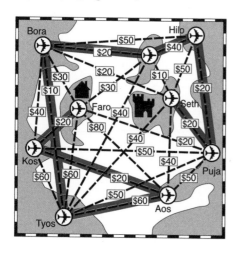

Gemstone Math (page 52)
There is 1 aquamarine, 2 zircons, 3 diamonds, 4 garnets, 5 sapphires, and 6 pearls.

Rich Riddle (page 52)
$387,420,489. Johnny could have thought of 9 to the 9th power, or 387,420,489.

Art Fair Stroll (page 53)
The order is: oil portraits, black and white photographs, watercolor, color photographs, quilt, pottery, windchimes, jewelry, lamps.

Remember Me? (Part I) (page 53)
Answer in Part 2.

Remember Me? (Part II) (page 54)

1. 9; 2. T; 3. 9; 4. L; 5. T

What's Flipped in Vegas, Stays in Vegas (page 54)
The coin came up heads 12 times.

Age Quandary (page 55)
66

Combined age in 12 years = 94.
$4 \times 12 = 48$, therefore, combined age now is $94 - 48 = 46$

In 5 years time the combined age is, therefore, $46 + 20 (4 \times 5) = 66$

Number Noggin-Scratcher (Part I) (page 55)

Answer in Part 2.

Number Noggin-Scratcher (Part II) (page 56)

B. 975

Maxims to Ponder (page 56)

1. Eagles may soar but weasels don't get sucked into jet engines.

2. Never argue with a spouse who is packing your parachute.

3. Never moon a werewolf.

Movie Mania (page 57)

	Movie	Cinema	Star
1	Lord Sings	Premiere	Bud Pott
2	Gladys Hater	Worldwide	Ross Crawe
3	Forest Chump	Screenz	Owen McAllen
4	Atlantic 11	Olympic	Tim Panks

Parade Parking (pages 58–59)

Times	License Plates	Locations	Brands
6:10 A.M.	BYS-81S	Racine Blvd.	Alfa Romeo
6:15 A.M.	XR6-192	First St.	Cadillac
6:20 A.M.	A14-S1D	Mitre Sq.	Subaru
6:25 A.M.	QE2-01C	Park St.	Isuzu
6:30 A.M.	JIB-P09	Bolero Ct.	Hyundai

Crypto-Logic (page 60)

GREAT

Try Saying This 3 Times Really Fast (page 60)

Wednesday

Globe Quest (page 61)

1. Miami

2. Dallas — 38

3. Chicago — 42

4. Atlanta — 38

5. New York — 22

6. Denver — 60

7. Los Angeles — 34

8. Phoenix — 42

9. Seattle — 22

TOTAL — 298

Race to the Truth (page 62)

The order is: Benedict, Tasha, John, Morgan, Laura, Jess, Kelsey

A Bright Idea (page 62)

He flipped a switch and filled the room with light.

Visualize This! (page 63)

Ditch, crossroads, hill, signpost, bridge, aqueduct, fence, wishing well, scarecrow, restaurant, canal lock, traffic lights

Stopping for Directions (Part I) (page 63)

Answer in Part 2.

Stopping for Directions (Part II) (page 64)

B

Apple Order (page 64)

550. .32x=176; x=176/.32

Globe Quest (page 65)

1. Miami — 34
2. New York — 45
3. Atlanta — 31
4. Chicago — 74
5. Phoenix — 75
6. Los Angeles — 25
7. Dallas — 36
8. Denver — 49
9. Seattle

TOTAL — 369

Top Scorers (pages 66–67)

Goals Scored	Player	Team	Town
23	Sean Stang	Mustangs	Playalinda
24	Lou Lilla	Cowboys	Smallville
25	Dale Dakota	Fighters	Vesuvius
26	Peter Paris	Giants	Madridge
27	Greg Greyson	Polar Bears	Harley

Gemstone Math (page 68)

The count is: 1 peridot, 2 rubies, 3 pearls, 4 garnets, 5 pieces of turquoise, and 6 agates.

Fill 'Er Up (page 68)

1. Fill bucket A; 2. fill bucket B from bucket A, filling B and leaving 5 gallons in A; 3. empty bucket B; 4. refill bucket B from bucket A, this leaves 1 gallon in bucket A; 5. empty bucket B and put the 1 gallon from A into B; 6. refill bucket A; 7. fill bucket B from bucket A—it will take 3 gallons, leaving 6 gallons in A

Spy Fly (page 69)

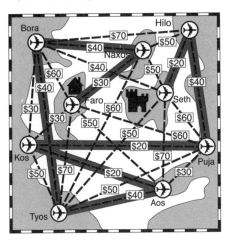

Crypto-Logic (page 70)

DONE

Sequence (page 70)

Go Dutch. The words start and end with successive letters of the alphabet – a, b, c, d, e, f, g, h

Name that Name (Part I) (page 71)

Answer in Part 2.

Name that Name (Part II) (page 72)

First Name	Surname	Profession
Tony	Sparrow	Entertainer
Samuel	Painter	Carpenter
Frank	Cook	Chauffeur
Samantha	Kitchen	Tailor
Alan	Wood	Baker
Annette	Driver	Cook
Julia	Singer	Ornithologist

Globe Quest (page 73)

1. Miami
2. Dallas — 35
3. Los Angeles — 22
4. Phoenix — 54
5. Denver — 66
6. Atlanta — 25
7. New York — 56
8. Chicago — 35
9. Seattle — 21

TOTAL — 314

Hockey Cards (pages 74-75)

Price	Collector	Player	Year
$40	Keaton	Harris	1983
$49	Jesse	Hansen	1989
$58	Reid	Hillstrand	1986
$67	Eddie	Colburn	1994
$76	Abe	Fourtner	1993

Mend the Bridges (page 76)

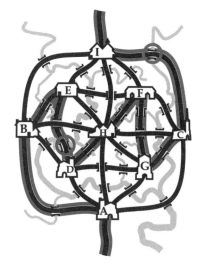

179

Spy Fly (page 77)

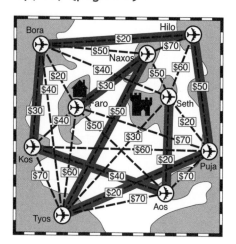

Spy Fly (page 81)

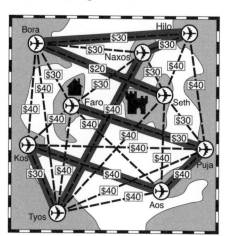

Publishing Poetry (pages 78–79)

Months	Authors	Titles	Editors
August	Dickens	Nine Takes	Valerie
September	Pennington	For Gerald	Marilyn
October	Farnsworth	California	Lyn
November	Beaufort	Driven Away	Jeff
December	Leary	Thieves City	Timothy

Crypto-Logic (page 80)

MAGIC. If S is 5 then M is 7, and U is 10. Therefore C is 6, and E is 3. So G is thereby 4, and A is 2. A plus G is 6, and 6 - 6 = 1 which is therefore zero.

Robber Riddle (page 80)

Why did the robber wear white gloves? He didn't want to be caught red-handed.

Visualize This! (page 82)

The order is: truck, ball, keyboard, abacus, Lego, action man, catapult, coloring book, racing car, teddy bear, xylophone, toy boat.

What Comes Next? (page 83)

1. H(ydrogen), H(elium), L(ithium), B(eryllium), B(oron), C(arbon), N(itrogen), O(xygen) Elements;

2. K(ingdom), P(hyllum), C(lass), O(rder), F(amily), G(enus), S(pecies) Taxonomy order;

3. P(arentheses), E(xponents), M(ultiply), D(ivide), A(dd), S(ubtract) Order of math operations

Number Noggin-Scratcher (Part 1) (page 83)

See part 2.

Number Noggin-Scratcher (Part II) (page 84)

D. 554

Lottery Logic (page 84)

Joe reached into his pocket and pulled out two more dollar bills. He added them to the pot, making the total $36.

Then the pot could be divided: Gary got one-half of $36, or $18; Hurley got one-third of $36, or $12; Joe got one-ninth of $36, or $4. $18 1 $12 1 $4 5 $34. Joe took the leftover $2 and put it back in his pocket.

Doggie Dinners (page 85)

C. 33. If one bag feeds 8 puppies, then 8 would feed 64. We need to feed only 20 puppies, leaving 64-20, or 44 puppies to be converted into dogs. Because puppes are a 4 to 3 ratio to dogs, the answer is 33.

Courier Confusion (Part I) (page 85)

See part 2.

Courier Confusion (Part II) (page 86)

Don Jensen
The Willows
4th Floor
94 Grand Oaks Avenue
Bakersfield,
CA 93301

Riddle (page 86)

Bernard and Colin were hurricanes.

Answer in the Round (page 87)

dining room table

Mend the Bridges (page 88)

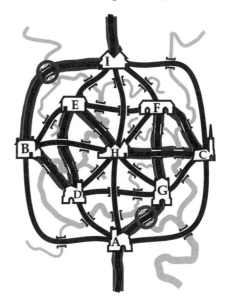

Spy Fly (page 89)

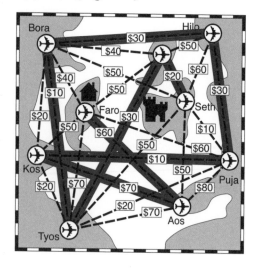

Crypto-Logic (page 90)

SIMPLIFY

Race to the Truth (page 90)

The order is: Tina, Lawrence, Kendra, Michaela, Salman, Dirk, Genevieve.

Gemstone Math (page 91)

The count is: 1 piece of jade, 2 amethysts, 3 rubies, 4 pieces of topaz, 5 garnets, 6 sapphires.

Mixed Figures (Part I) (page 91)

See part 2.

Mixed Figures (Part II) (page 92)

1. Triangle; 2. Five.

Word Columns (page 92)

"The vanity of being known to be trusted with a secret is generally one of the chief motives to disclose it."

Spy Fly (page 93)

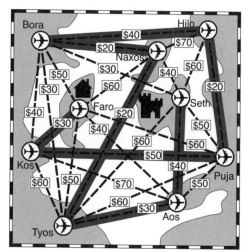

Appleton Arena (pages 94–95)

Day Of The Week	Home Team	Away Team	Game Time
Monday	Anglers	Raiders	4:00 P.M.
Tuesday	Bluebirds	Skaters	2:45 P.M.
Wednesday	Camelbacks	Penguins	2:30 P.M.
Thursday	Sharks	Twin	11:00 A.M.
Friday	Drafters	Marlins	1:45 P.M.

Name Calling (page 96)

CAVIAR

Name Calling (page 96)

When the house is swept, everything turns up.

Eat Your Veggies (Part I) (page 97)

See part 2.

Eat Your Veggies (Part II) (page 98)

Celery, corn, potatoes, bell peppers, broccoli, mushrooms, garlic

Race to the Truth (page 98)

The order is: Tony, Jonathan, Courtney, Patrice, Rob, Kenneth, Cameron.

Spy Fly (page 99)

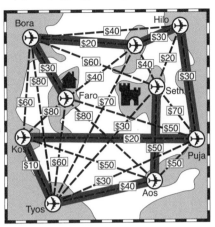

Crypto-Logic (page 100)

TRICKERY

Gemstone Math (page 100)

There are: 1 piece of jade, 2 of turquoise, 3 topazes, 4 pearls, 5 sapphires, and 6 rubies.

Globe Quest (page 101)

1. Miami		
2. Chicago	22
3. New York	48
4. Atlanta	68
5. Dallas	36
6. Phoenix	51
7. Los Angeles	39
8. Denver	24
9. Seattle	38
TOTAL	326

Stock Market Gains (pages 102–103)

Stock Prices	Symbols	Investors	Increases
$8.15	TTHP	Richard	+1.2%
$8.22	AMDQ	Carl	+1.9%
$8.29	DZZW	Pablo	+2.0%
$8.36	CPYL	Izzy	+2.6%
$8.43	MLVX	Ralph	+5.1%

Rook Jumping (page 104)

4	4 6	2 1	0 18 FINISH	4	3 0 START
2	4 11	4	4 15	1 14	4 10
1	5	1 2	3	4	1 9
5	3 5	2 3	3 17	3 4	5
2	4 7	5	5	2	2 8
2	3 12	4	2 16	4 13	5

Liar's Logic! (page 105)

Since A is telling the truth, we know C is lying when saying that B is a truth teller. Therefore D must be the second truth teller.

Number Jumble (pages 105–106)
6; 1; 7; 5.

Mend the Bridges (page 107)
Answers may vary.

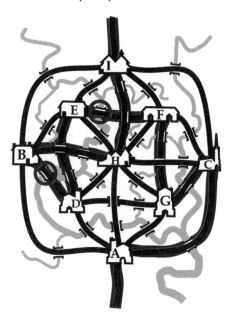

Globe Quest (page 108)

1. Miami	38
2. Dallas	35
3. New York	49
4. Atlanta	52
5. Denver	48
6. Chicago	32
7. Los Angeles	48
8. Phoenix	62
9. Seattle	
TOTAL	364

Overheard Information (Part I) (page 109)

See part 2.

Overheard Information (Part II) (page 110)

1. B. False; 2. B. False; 3. A. True; 4. A. True; 5. B. False.

Spy Fly (page 111)

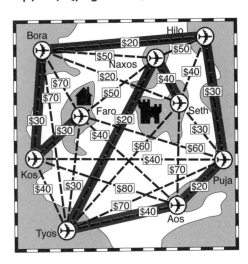

Crypto-Logic (page 112)

HOWEVER

Robber Riddle (page 112)

Why did the burglar open his sack when it started to rain?

He was hoping for some change in the weather.

Visualize This! (page 113)

Blue sock, jacket, belt, pants, red sock, tie, right gym shoe, cowboy hat, white shirt, left gym shoe, winter coat, boxer shorts, waistcoat

Arrows (Part I) (page 113)

See part 2.

Arrows (Part II) (page 114)

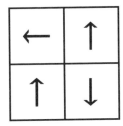

Gemstone Math (page 114)

The count is: 1 agate, 2 zircons, 3 rubies, 4 pearls, 5 amethysts, 6 sapphires, and 7 garnets.

Globe Quest (page 115)

1. Miami — 48
2. Atlanta — 48
3. Dallas — 41
4. Los Angeles — 47
5. Denver — 44
6. New York — 33
7. Chicago — 32
8. Phoenix — 47
9. Seattle —

TOTAL — 340

Bird Photography (pages 116-117)

Time	Birdwatcher	Photographs	Bird
6:30 A.M.	Victor	5	Scarlet Tanager
7:00 A.M.	Kevin	0	Titmouse
8:15 A.M.	Kaitlyn	29	Vulture
8:45 A.M.	Peter	12	Woodpecker
9:30 A.M.	Janice	3	Osprey

Mend the Bridges (page 118)

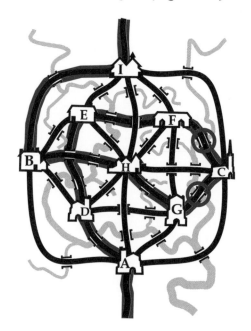

Liar's Logic! (page 119)

The liars are A and C. If A were telling the truth, B would have to be lying, making D and E liars as well (which is too many liars). This process of elimination leads to the answer that B, D, and E are the truth tellers.

Overheard Information (Part I) (page 119)

See part 2.

Overheard Information (Part II) (page 120)

1. B; 2. D; 3. A; D. 4. C

186

Don't Miss the Bus (Part I) (page 121)

See part 2.

Don't Miss the Bus (Part II) (page 122)

1. three; 2. stars; 3. the third row; 4. birdbath with birds in it; 5. QT; 6. behind his head; 7. mail carrier; 8. Math 5; 9. apple; 10. none

Globe Quest (page 123)

1. Miami	44
2. Dallas	28
3. Atlanta	20
4. New York	33
5. Chicago	40
6. Los Angeles	25
7. Phoenix	59
8. Denver	41
9. Seattle	
TOTAL	290

Crypto-Logic (page 124)

SWEET

Race to the Truth (page 124)

The order is: Geraldine, Chuck, Albert, Tiffany, Lorenzo, Mina, Dexter

Spy Fly (page 125)

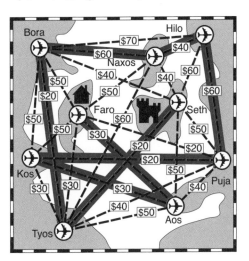

A Musical Discovery (page 126)

Year	Title	Instrument	Key
1863	Eliza	Violin	C minor
1864	Beatrice	Clarinet	D minor
1865	Heloise	Piano	A minor
1866	Margot	Cello	E minor
1867	Theresa	Flute	C major

Rook Jumping (page 128)

1 0 START	4 1	4	1 4	2 5	4
3	2 10	1 9	5	5	1
2	4	2	4	3 6	2
3 14	4 11	2 13	2 15	5	3 12
2	2 2	2	4 3	5	3
5 17	4	4 8	3 16	2 7	0 18 FINISH

A Passion for Fashion (Part I) (page 129)

See part 2.

A Passion for Fashion (Part II) (page 130)

Tank top, overalls, bell-bottoms, platform shoes, turtleneck sweater, cargo pants

Globe Quest (page 131)

1. Miami
2. Dallas — 50
3. New York — 27
4. Chicago — 35
5. Atlanta — 32
6. Denver — 28
7. Los Angeles — 27
8. Phoenix — 41
9. Seattle — 21

TOTAL — 261

Olympian Coaches (pages 132-133)

Year Joined	Coach	Olympics	Hockey Team
2001	Fred Heche	1984	Ozlanders
2002	Jim Welch	1998	Timberwolves
2003	Dyson Pyre	1980	Black Wings
2004	Adrian May	1994	Red Hawks
2005	Calvin Bash	1988	Kestrels

Equipment Mixup (pages 134-135)

Shoe Size	Player	Brand Name	Lace Color
9	Jonathan	Hockeymate	white
9.5	Michael	Ice-Pro	silver
10	Bryan	Chesterton	black
10.5	Nathaniel	Trembley	blue
11	Bennett	Slimline	gold

Sins & Virtues (page 136-137)

First Name	Last Name	Deadly Sin	Cardinal Virtue
Allison	Parker	Greed	Patience
Andrew	West	Pride	Diligence
Beth	Carlson	Gluttony	Chastity
Elliot	Severn	Sloth	Kindness
Harold	Brooks	Envy	Charity
Marcia	Holding	Lust	Temperance
Sofia	Lorenson	Wrath	Humility

Up in Smoke (page 138)

Robber Riddle (page 139)

Why was the thief all wet?
He tried to rob a riverbank.

Bookstore Browse (page 139)

The order is: biography, classics, science fiction, romance, travel, young adult, cookbooks.

Spy Fly (page 140)

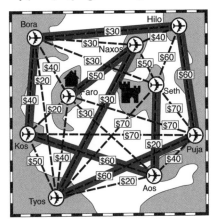

Crypto-Logic (page 141)
IMPROVE

Number Noggin-Scratcher (Part I) (page 141)

See part 2.

Number Noggin-Scratcher (Part II) (page 142)

D. 3456

Gemstone Math (page 142)
The count is: 1 turquoise, 2 amethysts, 3 diamonds, 4 opals, 5 pearls, 6 garnets, 7 pieces of jade, and 8 emeralds

Globe Quest (page 143)

1. Miami — 25
2. Chicago — 43
3. New York — 69
4. Dallas — 57
5. Atlanta — 24
6. Denver — 47
7. Los Angeles — 52
8. Phoenix — 33
9. Seattle —

TOTAL — 350

Hockey Schedule (pages 144–145)

Game Time	Home Team	Away Team	Channel
11:30 A.M.	Ewings	Ravens	ESPT II
1:00 P.M.	Coyotes	Timberwolves	THN
2:30 P.M.	Brahmins	Patriots	HLH
4:00 P.M.	Bees	Quests	ESPT I
5:30 P.M.	Dolphins	Sharks	STN

Spy Fly (page 146)

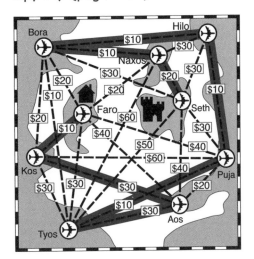

Rook Jumping (page 147)

1 0 START	**4** 1	**4**	**1** 4	**2** 5	**4**
3	**2** 10	**1** 9	**5**	**5**	**1**
2	**4**	**2**	**4** 6	**3**	**2**
3 14	**4** 11	**2** 13	**2** 15	**5**	**3** 12
2	**2** 2	**5**	**4** 3	**5**	**3**
5 17	**4**	**4** 8	**3** 16	**2** 7	**0** 18 FINISH

Liar's Logic! (page 151)

The liars are C and E. If C were telling the truth, E would have to be as well, and D, B and A would have to be lying (as D and B contradict C, and A agrees with B), and this would be too many liars. By such a process of elimination it becomes evident that the ones telling the truth are A, B and D. We can be sure of everyone's names.

Globe Quest (page 152)

1. Miami

2. Atlanta — 30

3. New York — 33

4. Chicago — 58

5. Los Angeles — 20

6. Denver — 31

7. Dallas — 21

8. Phoenix — 20

9. Seattle — 42

TOTAL — 255

Japanese Tea Shop (pages 148-149)

Prices	Customers	Teas	Amounts
$2.75/oz	Xander	Hojicha	5 ounces
$3.25/oz	Brian	Bancha	16 ounces
$3.75/oz	Matthew	Kukicha	12 ounces
$4.25/oz	Richard	Gyokuro	10 ounces
$4.75/oz	Uriel	Genmaicha	7 ounces

Mend the Bridges (page 150)

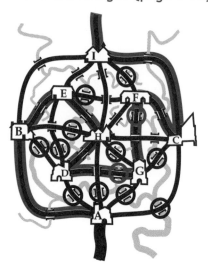

Spy Fly (page 153)

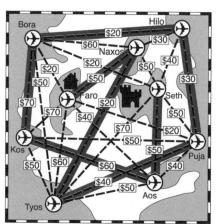

A Day at the Races (page 154)

Places	Owners	Pigs	Numbers
First	Terrence	Pinky	#3
Second	Paul	Hamlet	#11
Third	Emily	Squiggles	#9
Fourth	Kendra	Charlotte	#8
Fifth	Makenna	Rutager	#6

Robber Riddle (page 156)

Why did the thief only say "meow" to the police?

Because he was a cat burglar.

Restaurant Riddle (page 156)

The order is: sushi, burger joint, Mexican, Korean barbeque, pizza, ice cream parlor, sandwich place.

Gemstone Math (page 157)

There are: 1 diamond, 2 rubies, 3 emeralds, 4 garnets, 5 pearls, 6 amethysts, 7 sapphires, 8 opals.

Ante Up (page 157)
B. $19.00

Treasure Hunt (page 158)

The order is: London, Paris, Pretoria, Singapore, Cairo, Jakarta, Sydney, Buenos Aires, Rio de Janeiro

Not So Happy Birthday (page 159)

The date is January 1. Molly's birthday is December 31. Two days ago, on December 30 of last year, she was 39. That means today, she is 40. On December 31 of this year, she will turn 41. On December 31 of next year, she will turn 42. So next year, she really will be 42 and Homer will still be in the doghouse.

Number Noggin-Scratcher (Part I) (page 159)

Answer in part 2.

Number Noggin-Scratcher (Part II) (page 160)

C. 672

She's a Rich Girl (page 160)

Betty

Round and Round We Go (page 161)

EARTH, PIZZA, HELM, SOCCER BALL, STOPWATCH.

Globe Quest (page 163)

1. Miami	
	69
2. New York	
	45
3. Denver	
	47
4. Dallas	
	21
5. Atlanta	
	25
6. Chicago	
	35
7. Los Angeles	
	41
8. Phoenix	
	35
9. Seattle	
TOTAL	318

Crypto-Logic (page 164)

DECEPTIVE

Gemstone Math (page 164)

The count is: 1 opal, 2 aquamarines, 3 diamonds, 4 emeralds, 5 pearls, 6 amethysts, and 7 peridots.

Mend the Bridges (page 165)

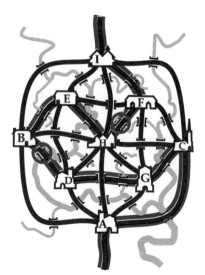

Science Stroll (page 166)

The order is: ant farm, miniature volcano, solar system model, miniature bridge, plant seedlings, robot, fossil exhibit, circuit board display

Spending Account (page 166)

She has $40 left.
$513 less $4/9$ ($228)=$285
$285 less 60% ($171)=$114
$114 less $74=$40

Good-Looking Logic (page 167)

Johnny Pitt installed his global positioning system in his attic.

George Cruise installed a robot vacuum in his living room.

Tom Depp installed a PC in his bathroom. Brad Damon installed a wide-screen TV in his bedroom.

Matt Clooney installed a DVD player in his kitchen.

Spy Fly (page 168)

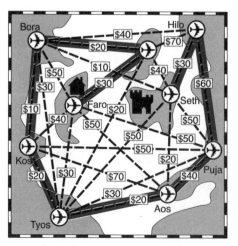